BUREAUCRACY
IN MODERN SOCIETY

STUDIES

IN SOCIOLOGY

Bureaucracy
in Modern Society

by PETER M. BLAU, *University of Chicago*

With a foreword by

CHARLES H. PAGE, *University of Massachusetts*

Random House

NEW YORK

THE MOUNTING interest of social scientists in the study of the structure and dynamics of bureaucracy has several sources. Most apparent is the unprecedented growth in modern society of large-scale formal organizations within which must be developed hierarchical administrative and operating social machinery, if their tasks are to be achieved. The pacesetters, of course, are big business and industry, big government, massive armed forces, and, in recent years, big labor; but bureaucracy's features mark more and more areas of modern life, including, for example, many associations devoted to education, scientific and scholarly pursuits, religion, social welfare, and recreation. These facts of changing social organization are inescapable for social scientist and layman alike.

The moral and political implications of these facts are a second source of interest in bureaucracy. Social scientists, no less than philosophers and artists and many less articulate witnesses—and "victims"—of bureaucracy's multisided thrust, are often deeply concerned with the presumed dangers of standardization and routinization, of impersonality and interchangeability, of bigness itself. These traits of bureaucracy are viewed in many quarters as an imposing threat to freedom, individualism, and spontaneity, cherished values in a liberal society. Such anxieties are not relieved, necessarily, by the recognition of the enormous accomplishments of man's "greatest social invention."

But many social scientists are, or become, social technicians. Managerial preoccupation with the improvement of organizational *efficiency*—whether the goal is the production of automobiles or the training of combat troops or the provision of social services or the education of young people—encourages the recruitment of personnel equipped with social research skills. And here is a third source of growing interest in bureaucracy. For these recruits are not only social technicians, providing immediately useful information for the managers of men and machines. In many cases, they maintain their scientific role, producing empirical studies, the findings of which, of course, may often serve managerial interests, but may also contribute to accumulative social theory. Thus the Hawthorne Western Electric studies, a landmark investigation of the 1930s, helped to revise the theoretical model of bureaucracy by demonstrating and documenting the role of various social factors in the operations of the plant, including heretofore obscure functions of informal groups and relationships. This study and subsequent reports of the informal and relatively spontaneous features of bureaucracy—in factories, governmental bureaus, military units, and elsewhere—have altered the ever formal model by establishing the positive functional contributions (not merely the dysfunctions) of "bureaucracy's other face."

Its informal face was known to Max Weber, although that great theorist's ideal scheme strongly accents bureaucracy's formal components. Weber's theoretical formulations in this subject, supported by the general prestige of his writings among American sociologists in recent years, constitute a further source of widespread interest in bureaucracy.

These several influences are evidenced in a rapidly expanding literature. Recent publications by Reinhard Bendix, Peter Blau, Robert Dubin, Alvin W. Gouldner, S. M. Lipset, Herbert A. Simon, and Philip Selznick (among others) represent efforts to test and refine theoretical propositions on the basis of empirical research. In 1952, R. K. Merton and his colleagues published a source book of readings,* containing an impressive sample of past and contemporary writings on diverse aspects of bureaucracy. These are sure signs that the serious study of the subject has come of age.

Professor Blau's Short Study is the first systematic sociological textbook on bureaucracy as such. In contrast with some pioneering textual ventures, however, *Bureaucracy in Modern Society* reveals, on the one hand, the author's close familiarity with the numerous and frequently fugitive contributions to the field and, on the other hand, keen insights derived from his own investigations. These qualities help to make this study a text of many merits: theoretical sophistication and conceptual precision; skillful and illuminating utilization of concrete materials—note especially the rewarding exploitation of case studies in the treatment of "Bureaucracy in Process"; clarity of exposition, free of unnecessary jargon and designed to hold the reader to the march of the analysis; economy of presentation, encouraging the student to read more widely in the field, a pursuit now abetted by the availability of an excellent source book.

Bureaucracy in Modern Society possesses a further virtue. For the author brings out sharply positive as well as negative functional interrelations between bureaucracy and democracy, some of which are by no means apparent. To be sure, Professor Blau aligns himself with democratic values. But his study, I believe, is a stimulating and valuable book for bureaucrats themselves, for bureaucracy's severest critics, and for both students and readers in general, more and more of whom today must man bureaucracy's posts.

CHARLES H. PAGE

* *Reader in Bureaucracy*, Glencoe, Ill.: Free Press, 1952. Merton's coeditors are Ailsa P. Gray, Barbara Hockey, and Hanan C. Selvin.

CONTENTS

BUREAUCRACY
IN MODERN SOCIETY

1

Why Study Bureaucracy?

"THAT STUPID BUREAUCRAT!" Who has not felt this way at one time or another? When we are sent from one official to the next without getting the information we want; when lengthy forms we had to fill out in sextuplicate are returned to us because we forgot to cross a "t" or dot an "i"; when our applications are refused on some technicality —that is when we think of bureaucracy. Colloquially, the term "bureaucracy" has become an epithet which refers to inefficiency and red tape in the government; but this was not its original meaning, and it is not the way the term will be used in this book.

If you alone had the job of collecting the dues in a small fraternity, you could proceed at your own discretion. But if five persons had this job in a large club, they would find it necessary to organize their work lest some members were asked for dues repeatedly and others never. If hundreds of persons have the assignment of collecting taxes from millions of citizens, their work must be very systematically organized; otherwise chaos would reign and the assignment could not be fulfilled. The type of organization designed to accomplish large-scale administrative tasks by systematically coordinating the work of many individuals is called a bureaucracy. This concept, then, applies to organizing principles that are intended to improve administrative efficiency and that generally do so, although bureaucratization occasionally has the opposite effect of producing inefficiency. Since complex administrative problems confront most large organizations, bureaucracy is not confined to the military and civilian branches of the government but is also found in business, unions, churches, universities, and even in baseball.

While the popular notion that bureaucracies are typically inefficient is not valid, this does not mean that the social scientist can simply dismiss it. The prevalence of this false belief in our society is a social fact that should be explained. In this study, after bureaucratic operations have been analyzed and clarified, such an explanation will be suggested in the last chapter. There we shall see that bureaucratization has implications in a democratic society that engender antagonism toward it. Whereas this antagonism usually results from the ruthless efficiency of bureaucracies, and not from their inefficiency, people often feel constrained to give vent to it by accusing bureaucracies of inefficiency, just as you might call a fellow who made you angry "stupid" even though it was not his lack of intelligence that aroused your anger.

The Rationalization of Modern Life

Much of the magic and mystery that used to pervade human life and lend it enchantment has disappeared from the modern world.* This is largely the price of rationalization. In olden times, nature was full of mysteries, and man's most serious intellectual endeavors were directed toward discovering the ultimate meaning of his existence. Today, nature holds fewer secrets for us. Scientific advances, however, have not only made it possible to explain many natural phenomena but have also channeled human thinking. Modern man is less concerned than, say, medieval man was with ultimate values and symbolic meanings, with those aspects of mental life that are not subject to scientific inquiry, such as religious truth and artistic creation. This is an age of great scientists and engineers, not of great philosophers or prophets.

The secularization of the world that spells its disenchantment is indicated by the large amount of time we spend in making a living and getting ahead, and the little time we spend in contemplation and religious activities. Compare the low prestige of moneylenders and the high prestige of priests in former eras with the very different positions of bankers and preachers today. Preoccupied with perfecting efficient means for achieving objectives, we tend to forget why we want to reach those goals. Since we neglect to clarify the basic values that determine why some objectives are preferable to others, objectives lose their significance, and their pursuit becomes an end in itself. This tendency is portrayed in Budd Shulberg's novel *What Makes Sammy Run?* The answer to the question in the title is that only running makes him run, because he is so busy trying to get ahead that he has no time to find out where he is going. Continuous striving for success is

* The disenchantment of the world is a main theme running through the writings of the German sociologist Max Weber, whose classical analysis of bureaucratic structure will be discussed presently.

not Sammy's means for the attainment of certain ends but the very goal of his life.

These consequences of rationalization have often been deplored, and some observers have even suggested that it is not worth the price.[1] There is no conclusive evidence, however, that alienation from profound values is the inevitable and permanent by-product of rationalization, and not merely an expression of its growing pains. The beneficial results of rationalization—notably the higher standard of living and the greater amount of leisure it makes possible, and the raising of the level of popular education it makes necessary—permit an increasing proportion of the population, not just a privileged elite, to participate actively in the cultural life of the society. This could ultimately lead to a flowering of the arts and other cultural pursuits on a wider scale than that in any earlier period.

Our high standard of living is usually attributed to the spectacular technological developments that have occurred since the Industrial Revolution, but this explanation ignores two related facts. First, the living conditions of most people during the early stages of industrialization, after they had moved from the land into the cities with their sweatshops, were probably much worse than they had been before. Dickens depicts these terrible conditions in certain novels, and Marx describes them in his biting critique of the capitalistic economy.[2] Second, major improvements in the standard of living did not take place until administrative procedures as well as the material technology had been revolutionized. Modern machines could not be utilized without the complex administrative machinery needed for running factories employing thousands of workers. It was not so much the invention of new machines as the introduction of mass-production methods that enabled Henry Ford to increase wages and yet produce a car so cheaply that it ceased to be a luxury. When

Ford later refused to make further administrative innovations, in the manner of his competitors, the position of his company suffered, but after his grandson instituted such changes the company manifested new competitive strength. Rationalization in administration is a prerequisite for the full exploitation of technological knowledge in mass production, and thus for a high standard of living.*

Let us examine some of the administrative principles on which the productive efficiency of the modern factory depends. If every worker manufactured a complete car, each would have to be a graduate of an engineering college, and even then he could not do a very good job, since it would be impossible for him to be at once an expert mechanical engineer, electrical engineer, and industrial designer. Besides, there would not be enough people with engineering degrees in the country to fill all the positions. Specialization permits the employment of many less-trained workers, which lowers production costs. Moreover, whereas the jack-of-all-trades is necessarily master of none, each employee can become a highly skilled expert in his particular field of specialization.

What has been taken apart must be put together again. A high degree of specialization creates a need for a complex system of coordination. No such need exists in the small shop, where the work is less specialized, all workers have direct contact with one another, and the boss can supervise the performance of all of them. The president of a large company cannot possibly discharge his man-

---

* To be sure, activities of trade unions have greatly contributed to the raising of our standard of living by forcing employers to distribute a larger proportion of their income to workers. Without administrative efficiency in the production and distribution of goods, however, there would be less income to distribute, and fewer goods could be bought with a given amount of income. Moreover, the strength of unions also depends on an efficient administrative machinery.

agerial responsibility for coordination through direct consultation with each one of several thousand workers.
Managerial responsibility, therefore, is exercised through
a hierarchy of authority, which furnishes lines of communication between top management and every employee
for obtaining information on operations and transmitting
operating directives. (Sometimes, these lines of communication become blocked, and this is a major source of inefficiency in administration.)

Effective coordination requires disciplined performance,
which cannot be achieved by supervision alone but must
pervade the work process itself. This is the function of
rules and regulations that govern operations whether they
specify the dimensions of nuts and bolts or the criteria to
be used in promoting subordinates. Even in the ideal case
where every employee is a highly intelligent and skilled
expert, there is a need for disciplined adherence to regulations. Say one worker had discovered that he could produce bolts of superior quality by making them one-eighth
of an inch larger, and another worker had found that he
could increase efficiency by making nuts one-eighth of an
inch smaller. Although each one made the most rational
decision in terms of his own operations, the nuts and bolts
would of course be useless because they would not match.
How one's own work fits together with that of others is
usually far less obvious than in this illustration. For the
operations of hundreds of employees to be coordinated,
each individual must conform to prescribed standards even
in situations where a different course of action appears to
him to be most rational. This is a requirement of all teamwork, although in genuine teamwork the rules are not
imposed from above but are based on common agreement.

Efficiency also suffers when emotions or personal considerations influence administrative decisions. If the owner
of a small grocery expands his business and opens a

second store, he may put his son in charge even though another employee is better qualified for the job. He acts on the basis of his personal attachment rather than in the interest of business efficiency. Similarly, an official in a large company might not promote the best-qualified worker to foreman if one of the candidates were his brother. Indeed, his personal feelings could prevent him from recognizing that the qualifications of his brother were inferior. Since the subtle effects of strong emotions cannot easily be suppressed, the best way to check their interference with efficiency is to exclude from the administrative hierarchy those interpersonal relationships that are characterized by emotional attachments. While relatives sometimes work for the same company, typically they are not put in charge of one another. Impersonal relationships assure the detachment necessary if efficiency alone is to govern administrative decisions. However, relationships between employees who have frequent social contacts do not remain purely impersonal, as we shall see.

These four factors—specialization, a hierarchy of authority, a system of rules, and impersonality—are the basic characteristics of bureaucratic organization. Factories are bureaucratically organized, as are government agencies, and if this were not the case they could not operate efficiently on a large scale. Chapter Two is devoted to a more detailed analysis of bureaucratic structure and the conditions that give rise to bureaucratization. But actual operations do not exactly follow the formal blueprint. To understand how bureaucracies function, we must observe them in action. This is the task of Chapters Three and Four, which are concerned, respectively, with bureaucratic work groups and relationships of authority. After discussing the internal structure and functioning of bureaucracies, we shall turn in the final two chapters to their implications for the society of which they are a part.

Specifically, we shall examine the consequences of bureaucratization for social change and for democracy. First,
however, the question raised in the title of this introduc-
tory chapter should be answered: why study bureaucracy?

The Value of Studying Bureaucracy

Learning to understand bureaucracies is more important
today than it ever was. It is, besides, of special significance
in a democracy. Finally, the study of bureaucratic organization makes a particular contribution to the advancement
of sociological knowledge.

Today Bureaucracy is not a new phenomenon. It
existed in rudimentary forms thousands of years ago in
Egypt and Rome. But the trend toward bureaucratization
has greatly accelerated during the last century. In contemporary society bureaucracy has become a dominant institution, indeed, the institution that epitomizes the modern
era. Unless we understand this institutional form, we cannot understand the social life of today.

The enormous size of modern nations and the organizations within them is one reason for the spread of bureaucracy. In earlier periods, most countries were small, even
large ones had only a loose central administration, and
there were few formal organizations except the government. Modern countries have many millions of citizens,
vast armies, giant corporations, huge unions, and numerous large voluntary associations.[3] To be sure, large size is
not synonymous with bureaucratic organization. However,
the problems posed by administration on a large scale tend
to lead to bureaucratization. As a matter of fact, the large
organizations that persisted longest in antiquity and even
survived this period, the Roman Empire and the Catholic
Church, were thoroughly bureaucratized.

In the United States, employment statistics illustrate the trend toward large, bureaucratic organizations. The federal government employed 8000 civil servants in 1820, a quarter of a million fifty years ago, and ten times that number today. If the men in military service are added, nearly 10 per cent of the American labor force, six million people, are in the employ of the federal government. Still larger is the number who work for large-scale private concerns, the extreme example being the American Telephone and Telegraph Company with three-quarters of a million employees. More than three-quarters of the employees in manufacturing work for firms with one hundred or more employees, and even in the retail trades, the bulwark of small business, one-sixth of all employees work for firms of the same size.

A large and increasing proportion of the American people spend their working lives as small cogs in the complex mechanisms of bureaucratic organizations. And this is not all, for bureaucracies also affect much of the rest of our lives. The employment agency we approach to get a job, and the union we join to protect it; the supermarket and the chain store where we shop; the school our children attend, and the political parties for whose candidates we vote; the fraternal organization where we play, and the church where we worship—all these more often than not are large organizations of the kind that tends to be bureaucratically organized.

In a Democracy Bureaucracy, as the foremost theoretician on the subject points out, "is a power instrument of the first order—for the one who controls the bureaucratic apparatus." [4]

Under normal conditions, the power position of a fully developed bureaucracy is always overtowering. The "political master" finds himself in the position of the "dilettante" who stands opposite the "expert," facing the trained official who stands within the management of administration. This holds whether the "master" whom the bureaucracy serves is a "people," equipped with the weapons of "legislative initiative," the "referendum," and the right to remove officials, or a parliament, elected on a . . . "democratic" basis and equipped with the right to vote a lack of confidence, or with the actual authority to vote it.[5]

Totalitarianism is the polar case of such bureaucratic concentration of power that destroys democratic processes, but not the only one. The same tendency can be observed in political machines that transfer the power that legally belongs to voters to political bosses, in business corporations that vest the power that rightfully belongs to stockholders in corporation officials, and in those unions that bestow the power that rightfully belongs to rank-and-file members upon union leaders. These cases lead some writers to contend that the present trend toward bureaucratization spells the doom of democratic institutions. This may well be too fatalistic a viewpoint, but there can be no doubt that this trend constitutes a challenge. To protect ourselves against this threat, while continuing to utilize these efficient administrative mechanisms, we must first learn fully to understand how bureaucracies function. Knowledge alone is not power, but ignorance surely facilitates subjugation. This is the reason why the study of bureaucratic organization has such great significance in a democracy.

The problem of efficiency versus democracy, which will occupy us at length later, can initially be clarified by distinguishing three types of association. If an association among men is established for the explicit purpose of producing jointly certain end-products, whether it is manufacturing cars or winning wars, considerations of efficiency are of primary importance; hence bureaucratization will further the achievement of this objective. However, if an association is established for the purpose of finding intrinsic satisfaction in common activities, say in religious worship, considerations of efficiency are less relevant. When such an association, for instance a religious body, grows so large that administrative problems engender bureaucratization, the pursuit of the original objectives may, indeed, be hampered.[6] Finally, if an association is established for the purpose of deciding upon common goals and courses of action to implement them, which is the function of democratic government (but not that of government agencies), the free expression of opinion must be safeguarded against other considerations, including those of efficiency. Since bureaucratization prevents the attainment of this objective, it must be avoided at all cost. Ideally, organizations of the first type would always be bureaucratized, and those of the last type, never. But one of the difficulties is that many organizations, such as unions, are of a mixed type.

For Sociologists The study of bureaucratic organization is of special significance for sociologists because it helps them in their task of finding an order in the complex interdependencies of social phenomena. The sociologist is concerned with explaining patterns of human behavior in terms of relationships between people and shared normative beliefs of people. For example, to explain why some students get poorer grades than others who are no more intelligent, this sociological hypothesis could be advanced: the former have fewer friends and the discomfort of their social isolation interferes with their work. Let us assume we would actually find that the grades of isolated students are lower than those of the rest. Would that prove the hypothesis? By no means, since the difference could be due to the fact that students who appear stupid in class become

less popular, or that radicals (or any other group) are
discriminated against by teachers and are also disliked by
fellow students.

This problem can be solved in the controlled experiment,
which makes it possible to demonstrate that a specific
factor has certain effects because all other factors are held
constant. If two test tubes have exactly the same content
and are kept under the same conditions except that one is
heated, the changes that occur in one liquid but not in the
other must be the result of heat. Many social conditions,
however, in contrast to most physical conditions, cannot
be duplicated in the laboratory. Although we can make
human subjects feel isolated in an experimental session,
this is not the same experience as having no friends in college, and other social conditions, such as international
warfare, cannot be reproduced in the laboratory at all.
This is a dilemma of social research: controlled conditions
are required for the testing of hypotheses, but the artificial
situation in laboratory experiments is usually not suitable
for this purpose. Not that this is an insurmountable dif-
ficulty; techniques have been devised to approximate the
analytical model of the controlled experiment outside the
laboratory. Still, the larger the number of varying factors
in the social situation, the smaller is the chance that explanatory hypotheses can be confirmed.

Bureaucracy provides, as it were, a natural laboratory
for social research. The formal organization, with its explicit regulations and official positions, constitutes controlled conditions, and these controls have not been artifi-
cially introduced by the scientist but are an inherent part
of the bureaucratic structure. To be sure, the daily activities and interactions of the members of a bureaucracy
cannot be entirely accounted for by the official blueprint.
If they could, there would be no need for conducting empirical studies in bureaucracies, since everything about

them could be learned by examining organizational charts and procedure manuals. Several factors in addition to official requirements influence daily operations, which means, of course, that conditions are not as fully controlled as in a laboratory experiment. Nevertheless, the explicit formal organization, the characteristics of which can be easily ascertained, reduces the number of variable conditions in the bureaucratic situation and thereby facilitates the search for and the testing of explanatory hypotheses.

In summary, the prevalence of bureaucracies in our society furnishes a practical reason for studying them; the fact that they endanger democratic institutions supplies an ideological reason; and the contribution their study can make to sociological knowledge provides a scientific reason for undertaking this task.

2

Theory and Development
of Bureaucracy

ADVANCEMENT in any science depends on developments in both theory and empirical research and on a close connection between them. The objectives of science are to improve the accuracy and scope of explanations of phenomena as a basis for better predictability and control. A system of interrelated explanatory propositions is a scientific theory. Not every insight, however, is a scientific proposition; this term refers only to those that have been confirmed in systematic research or can at least be confirmed in future research, which is not the case for all explanations. Toynbee's interpretation of history in terms of challenge and response, for instance, although it may provide new insights into the course of history, cannot be empirically tested, since there is no conceivable factual

evidence that would clearly disprove it. An important
methodological principle of science holds that only those
propositions can be empirically confirmed that indicate
precisely the evidence necessary for disproving them.

If undisciplined speculating does not further the advancement of science, neither does random data-collecting.
A large number of miscellaneous facts contribute as little
to the building of systematic theory as a large number of
odd stones contribute to the building of a house. To be
sure, unsophisticated fact-finding has its uses, and so does
undisciplined imagination, but for empirical research and
theoretical insights to serve science, they must be integrated. This requires that theory be precise enough to
direct research, and that research be oriented toward
establishing theoretical generalizations.

The lesson to be learned from these considerations is
that the study of bureaucracy should be governed by a
theoretical orientation and should focus upon the investigation of empirical cases. These case studies of bureaucracies, in turn, will help to clarify and refine our theoretical
understanding of this social structure and its functioning.
Following this procedure, we shall start with Max Weber's
famous theory of bureaucracy.

The Concept of Bureaucracy

The main characteristics of a bureaucratic structure (in
the "ideal-typical" case*), according to Weber, are the
following:

1. "The regular activities required for the purposes of
the organization are distributed in a fixed way as official
duties." [1] The clear-cut division of labor makes it possible
to employ only specialized experts in each particular posi-

* The "ideal type" is discussed later in this chapter.

tion and to make every one of them responsible for the effective performance of his duties. This high degree of specialization has become so much part of our socio-economic life that we tend to forget that it did not prevail in former eras but is a relatively recent bureaucratic innovation.

2. "The organization of offices follows the principle of hierarchy; that is, each lower office is under the control and supervision of a higher one." [2] Every official in this administrative hierarchy is accountable to his superior for his subordinates' decisions and actions as well as his own. To be able to discharge his responsibility for the work of subordinates, he has authority over them, which means that he has the right to issue directives and they have the duty to obey them. This authority is strictly circumscribed and confined to those directives that are relevant for official operations. The use of status prerogatives to extend the power of control over subordinates beyond these limits does not constitute the legitimate exercise of bureaucratic authority.

3. Operations are governed "by a consistent system of abstract rules . . . [and] consist of the application of these rules to particular cases." [3] This system of standards is designed to assure uniformity in the performance of every task, regardless of the number of persons engaged in it, and the coordination of different tasks. Hence explicit rules and regulations define the responsibility of each member of the organization and the relationships between them. This does not imply that bureaucratic duties are necessarily simple and routine. It must be remembered that strict adherence to general standards in deciding specific cases characterizes not only the job of the file clerk but also that of the Supreme Court justice. For the former, it may involve merely filing alphabetically; for the latter, it involves interpreting the law of the land in

order to settle the most complicated legal issues. Bureaucratic duties range in complexity from one of these ex-
tremes to the other.

4. "The ideal official conducts his office . . . [in] a
spirit of formalistic impersonality, *'Sine ira et studio,'*
without hatred or passion, and hence without affection or
enthusiasm." [4] For rational standards to govern operations
without interference from personal considerations, a detached approach must prevail within the organization and
especially toward clients. If an official develops strong
feelings about some subordinates or clients, he can hardly
help letting those feelings influence his official decisions.
As a result, and often without being aware of it himself,
he might be particularly lenient in evaluating the work of
one of his subordinates or might discriminate against
some clients and in favor of others. The exclusion of personal considerations from official business is a prerequisite
for impartiality as well as for efficiency. The very factors
that make a government bureaucrat unpopular with his
clients, an aloof attitude and a lack of genuine concern
with their problems, actually benefit these clients. Disin-
terestedness and lack of personal interest go together. The
official who does not maintain social distance and becomes
personally interested in the cases of his clients tends to be
partial in his treatment of them, favoring those he likes
over others. Impersonal detachment engenders equitable
treatment of all persons and thus fosters democracy in
administration.

5. Employment in the bureaucratic organization is based
on technical qualifications and is protected against arbitrary dismissal. "It constitutes a career. There is a system
of 'promotions' according to seniority or to achievement,
or both." [5] These personnel policies, which are found not
only in civil service but also in many private companies,

encourage the development of loyalty to the organization and *esprit de corps* among its members. The consequent identification of employees with the organization motivates them to exert greater efforts in advancing its interests. It may also give rise to a tendency to think of themselves as a class apart from and superior to the rest of the society. Among civil servants, this tendency has been more pronounced in Europe, notably in Germany, than in the United States, but among military officers, it may be found here, too.

6. "Experience tends universally to show that the purely bureaucratic type of administrative organization . . . is, from a purely technical point of view, capable of attaining the highest degree of efficiency." [6] "The fully developed bureaucratic mechanism compares with other organizations exactly as does the machine with non-mechanical modes of production." [7] Bureaucracy solves the distinctive organizational problem of maximizing organizational efficiency, not merely that of individuals.

The superior administrative efficiency of bureaucracy is the expected result of its various characteristics as outlined by Weber. For an individual to work efficiently, he must have the necessary skills and apply them rationally and energetically; but for an organization to operate efficiently, more is required. Every one of its members must have the expert skills needed for the performance of his tasks. This is the purpose of specialization and of employment on the basis of technical qualifications, often ascertained by objective tests. Even experts, however, may be prevented by personal bias from making rational decisions. The emphasis on impersonal detachment is intended to eliminate this source of irrational action. But individual rationality is not enough. If the members of the organization were to make rational decisions independently, their

work would not be coordinated and the efficiency of the
organization would suffer. Hence there is need for discipline to limit the scope of rational discretion, which is met
by the system of rules and regulations and the hierarchy
of supervision. Moreover, personnel policies that permit
employees to feel secure in their jobs and to anticipate advancements for faithful performance of duties discourage
attempts to impress superiors by introducing clever innovations, which may endanger coordination. Lest this
stress on disciplined obedience to rules and rulings undermine the employee's motivation to devote his energies to
his job, incentives for exerting effort must be furnished.
Personnel policies that cultivate organizational loyalty and
that provide for promotion on the basis of merit serve this
function. In other words, the combined effect of bureaucracy's characteristics is to create social conditions which
constrain each member of the organization to act in ways
that, whether they appear rational or otherwise from his
individual standpoint, further the rational pursuit of
organizational objectives.

Without explicitly stating so, Weber supplies a *functional*
analysis of bureaucracy. In this type of analysis, a social
structure is explained by showing how each of its elements
contributes to its persistence and effective operations. Concern with discovering all these contributions, however,
entails the danger that the scientist may neglect to investigate the disturbances that various elements produce in
the structure. As a result, his presentation may make the
social structure appear to function more smoothly than it
actually does, since he neglects the disruptions that do in
fact exist. To protect ourselves against this danger, it is
essential to extend the analysis beyond the mere consideration of functions, as Robert K. Merton points out.[8] Of
particular importance for avoiding false implications of
stability and for explaining social change is the study of

dysfunctions, those consequences that interfere with adjustment and create problems in the structure.[9]

A re-examination of the foregoing discussion of bureaucratic features in the light of the concept of dysfunction reveals inconsistencies and conflicting tendencies. If reserved detachment characterizes the attitudes of the members of the organization toward one another, it is unlikely that high *esprit de corps* will develop among them. The strict exercise of authority in the interest of discipline induces subordinates, anxious to be highly thought of by their superiors, to conceal defects in operations from superiors, and this obstruction of the flow of information upward in the hierarchy impedes effective management. Insistence on conformity also tends to engender rigidities in official conduct and to inhibit the rational exercise of judgment needed for efficient performance of tasks. If promotions are based on merit, many employees will not experience advancements in their careers; if they are based primarily on seniority so as to give employees this experience and thereby to encourage them to become identified with the organization, the promotion system will not furnish strong incentives for exerting efforts and excelling in one's job. These illustrations suffice to indicate that the same factor that enhances efficiency in one respect often threatens it in another; it may have *both* functional and dysfunctional consequences.

Weber was well aware of such contradictory tendencies in the bureaucratic structure. But since he treats dysfunctions only incidentally, his discussion leaves the impression that administrative efficiency in bureaucracies is more stable and less problematical than it actually is. In part, it was his intention to present an idealized image of bureaucratic structure, and he used the conceptual tool appropriate for this purpose. Let us critically examine this conceptual tool.

Implications of the Ideal-Type Construct

Weber dealt with bureaucracy as what he termed an "ideal type." This methodological concept does not represent an average of the attributes of all existing bureaucracies (or other social structures), but a pure type, derived by abstracting the most characteristic bureaucratic aspects of all known organizations. Since perfect bureaucratization is never fully realized, no empirical organization corresponds exactly to this scientific construct.

The criticism has been made that Weber's analysis of an imaginary ideal type does not provide understanding of concrete bureaucratic structures. But this criticism obscures the fact that the ideal-type construct is intended as a guide in empirical research, not as a substitute for it. By indicating the characteristics of bureaucracy in its pure form, it directs the researcher to those aspects of organizations that he must examine in order to determine the extent of their bureaucratization. This is the function of all conceptual schemes: to specify the factors that must be taken into consideration in investigations and to define them clearly.

The ideal type, however, is not simply a conceptual scheme. It includes not only definitions of concepts but also generalizations about the relationships between them, specifically the hypothesis that the diverse bureaucratic characteristics increase administrative efficiency. Whereas conceptual definitions are presupposed in research and not subject to verification by research findings, hypotheses concerning relationships between factors are subject to such verification. Whether strict hierarchical authority, for example, in fact furthers efficiency is a question of empirical fact and not one of definition. But as a scientific construct, the ideal type cannot be refuted by empirical evidence. If a study of several organizations were to find that strict hierarchical authority is not related to efficiency, this would not prove that no such relationship exists in the ideal-type bureaucracy; it would show only that these organizations are not fully bureaucratized. Since generalizations about idealized states defy testing in systematic research, they have no place in science. On the other hand, if empirical evidence is taken into consideration and generalizations are modified accordingly, we deal with prevailing tendencies in bureaucratic structures and no longer with a pure type.

Two misleading implications of the ideal-type conception of bureaucracy deserve special mention. The student of social organization is concerned with the patterns of activities and interactions that reveal how social conduct is organized, and not with exceptional deviations from these patterns. The fact that one official becomes excited and shouts at his colleague, or that another arrives late at the office, is unimportant in understanding the organization, except that the rare occurrence of such events indicates that they are idiosyncratic, differing from the prevailing patterns. Weber's decision to treat only the purely formal organization of bureaucracy implies that all deviations from these formal requirements are idiosyncratic and of no interest for the student of organization. Recent empirical studies have shown this approach to be misleading. Informal relations and unofficial practices develop among the members of bureaucracies and assume an organized form without being officially sanctioned. Chester I. Barnard, one of the first to call attention to this phenomenon, held that these "informal organizations are necessary to the operations of formal organizations." [10] These informal patterns, in contrast to exceptional occurrences, as we shall see in Chapter Three, are a regular part of bureaucratic organizations and therefore must be taken into account in their analysis.

Weber's approach also implies that any deviation from the formal structure is detrimental to administrative efficiency. Since the ideal type is conceived as the perfectly efficient organization, all differences from it must necessarily interfere with efficiency. There is considerable evidence that suggests the opposite conclusion; informal relations and unofficial practices often contribute to efficient operations. In any case, the significance of these unofficial patterns for operations cannot be determined in advance on theoretical grounds but only on the basis of factual investigations. Before examining such case studies of bureaucracies it is useful to explore the conditions that give rise to bureaucratization.

Conditions that Give Rise to Bureaucratization

To say that there is a historical trend toward bureaucracy is to state that many organizations change from less to more bureaucratic forms of administration. Yet the historical trend itself and the changes in any specific organization are different phenomena. Both are expressions of the process of bureaucratization, but since different conditions account for them, they will be discussed separately.

Historical Conditions   One of the historical conditions that favors the development of bureaucracy is a money economy. This is not an absolute prerequisite. Bureaucracies based on compensation in kind existed, for example, in Egypt, Rome, and China. Generally, however, a money economy permits the payment of regular salaries, which, in turn, creates the combination of dependence and independence that is most conducive to the faithful performance of bureaucratic duties. Unpaid volunteers are too independent of the organization to submit unfailingly to its discipline. Slaves, on the other hand, are too dependent on their masters to have the incentive to assume responsibilities and carry them out on their own initiative. The economic dependence of the salaried employee on his job and his freedom to advance himself in his career engender the orientation toward work required for disciplined *and* responsible conduct. Consequently, there were few bureaucracies prior to the development of a monetary system and the abolition of slavery.

It has already been mentioned that sheer size encourages the development of bureaucracies, since they are mechanisms for executing large-scale administrative tasks. The large modern nation, business, or union is more likely to be bureaucratized than was its smaller counterpart in the past. More important than size as such, however, is the emergence of special administrative problems. Thus in ancient Egypt the complex job of constructing and regulating waterways throughout the country gave rise to the first known large-scale bureaucracy in history. In other countries, notably those with long frontiers requiring defense, bureaucratic methods were introduced to solve the problem of organizing an effective army and the related one of raising taxes for this purpose. England, without land frontiers, maintained only a small army in earlier centuries, which may in part account for the fact that the trend toward bureaucratization was less pronounced there than in continental nations, which had to support large armies. Weber cites the victory of the Puritans under the leadership of Cromwell over the Cavaliers, who fought more heroically but with less discipline, as an illustration of the superior effectiveness of a bureaucratized army.[11]

The capitalistic system also has furthered the advance of bureaucracy. The rational estimation of economic risks, which is presupposed in capitalism, requires that the regular processes of the competitive market not be interrupted by external forces in unpredictable ways. Arbitrary actions of political tyrants interfere with the rational calculation of gain or loss, and so do banditry, piracy, and social upheavals. The interest of capitalism demands, therefore, not only the overthrow of tyrannical rulers but also the establishment of governments strong enough to maintain order and stability. Note that after the American Revolution such representatives of the capitalists as Alexander Hamilton advocated a strong federal government, while representatives of farmers, in the manner of Jefferson, favored a weak central government.

Capitalism then promotes effective and extensive operations of the government. It also leads to bureaucratization in other spheres. The expansion of business firms and the consequent removal of most employees from activities directly governed by the profit principle make it increasingly necessary to introduce bureaucratic methods of administration for the sake of efficiency. These giant corporations, in turn, constrain workers, who no longer can bargain individually with an employer they know personally, to organize into large unions with complex administrative machineries. Strange as it may seem, the free-enterprise system fosters the development of bureaucracy in the government, in private companies, and in unions.

These historical conditions were not causes of bureaucracy in the usual sense of the term. Evidently, a large and effective army did not cause bureaucracy; on the contrary, bureaucratic methods of operation produced an effective large army. The need for these methods, however, arose in the course of trying to build such an army without them and helped bring about a bureaucratic form of organization. The qualifying word "helped" is essential. If needs inevitably created ways of meeting them, human society would be paradise. In this world, wishes are not horses, and beggars do not ride. Social needs, just as individual ones, often persist without being met. Knowledge of the conditions that engendered a need for bureaucracy does not answer the question: what made its development actually possible under some circumstances and not under others? The Cavaliers were in need of a better fighting force, as their defeat demonstrates. Why was it not they but the Puritans who organized a disciplined army?

In *The Protestant Ethic and the Spirit of Capitalism,* Weber indirectly answers this question. He shows that the Reformation—especially Calvinism, the religious doctrine of the Puritans—apart from its spiritual significance, had the social consequence of giving rise to this-worldly asceticism, a disciplined devotion to hard work in the pursuit of one's vocation. The Protestant has no Pope or priest to furnish spiritual guidance and absolve him for his sins, but must ultimately rely on his own conscience and faith; this encourages the emergence of self-imposed discipline. The strong condemnation of pleasure and emotions, exemplified by the Puritan "blue laws," generates the sobriety and detachment conducive to rational conduct. Moreover, in contrast to Catholicism and even Lutheranism, Calvinism does not emphasize that the existing order is God's creation but that it has been corrupted by man's sinfulness. Man's religious duty is not to adapt to this wicked world, nor to withdraw from it into a monastery, but to help transform it *pro gloriam Dei* through methodical efforts in his everyday life and regular work. The anxieties aroused by the doctrine of double predestination, according to which man cannot affect his predestined fate or even know whether he will be saved or damned, rein-

forced the Calvinist's tendency to adopt a rigorous discipline and immerse himself in his work as a way of relieving
his anxieties.

Protestantism, therefore, has transplanted the ascetic
devotion to disciplined hard work (which must be distinguished from the exertion of effort as a means for
reaching specific ends) from monastic life, to which it
was largely confined earlier, to the mundane affairs of
economic life. Although the explicit purposes of the Reformation were other-worldly and not this-worldly, the
psychological orientation it created had the unanticipated
consequence of helping to revolutionize the secular world.
For without this orientation toward ceaseless effort and
rational conduct as intrinsic moral values, Weber argues
convincingly, capitalism could not have come into existence, and neither, it should be added, could full-blown
bureaucracy have developed, because it too depends on
rational discipline.[12]

Structural Conditions The historical conditions that
led to the pervasiveness of bureaucracy today do not, of
course, explain why some organizations in contemporary
society are highly bureaucratized and others are not. These
variations raise the problem of the conditions within a
given social structure that give rise to its bureaucratization.
A recent empirical study is concerned with this problem.

Alvin W. Gouldner investigated the process of bureaucratization in a gypsum plant.[13] After the death of the old
manager, the company that owned the plant appointed a
man who had been in charge of one of its smaller factories
as his successor. The new manager, anxious to prove himself worthy of the promotion by improving productivity,
was faced with special difficulties. He was not familiar
with the ways of working that had become customary in
this plant, had not established informal relations with

his subordinates, and did not command the allegiance of workers, who still felt loyal to his predecessor. To marshal the willing support of workers and induce them to identify with his managerial objectives, he attempted to cultivate informal relations with them; but this cannot be done overnight. In the meantime, he found it necessary to discharge his managerial responsibilities by resorting to formal procedures. In the absence of informal channels of communication to keep him informed about the work situation, the new manager instituted a system of regular operational reports for this purpose. Since he did not know the workers well enough to trust them, he closely checked on their operations and ordered his lieutenants to establish strict discipline. When some of these lieutenants, used to the more lenient ways of the former manager, failed to adopt rigorous methods of close supervision, he replaced them by outsiders who were more sympathetic with his disciplinarian approach. These innovations alienated workers and deepened the gulf between them and the manager, with the result that he had to rely increasingly on formal bureaucratic methods of administration.

> The role of the successor . . . confronted Peele with distinctive problems. He had to solve these problems if he wished to hold his job as manager. In the process of solving them, the successor was compelled to use bureaucratic methods. Peele intensified bureaucracy not merely because he wanted to, not necessarily because he liked bureaucracy, nor because he valued it above other techniques, but also because he was constrained to do so by the tensions of his succession.[14]

In the interest of his objective of gaining control over the operations in the plant, it was necessary for the successor to introduce bureaucratic procedures. At the same time, for workers to realize their objective of maintaining some independent control over their own work, it was

necessary for them to oppose the introduction of disciplinarian measures. As noted above, the existence of a need
does not explain why it is met. In this case, two conflicting needs existed side by side, with the "victor" determined
by the power structure in the organization. The powerful
position of the manager was responsible for his ability to
meet his need by bureaucratizing operations, as indicated
by the following comparison with a situation where he was
not similarly successful.

This plant consisted of a gypsum mine and a wallboard
factory, but the process of bureaucratic formalization was
confined to the factory. Stronger informal ties and more
pronounced group solidarity prevailed among miners than
among factory workers, partly as a consequence of the
common danger to which they were exposed in the mine.
Miners were highly motivated to work hard, and they had
developed their own unofficial system of assigning tasks
among themselves; for instance, new miners had to do the
dirty jobs. Hence there was less need in the mine for
formal discipline and rules prescribing exact duties. Nevertheless, Peele attempted to formalize operating procedures
there, too. The strength of their informal organization,
however, made it possible for miners, in contrast to factory workers, effectively to resist these attempts. The
process of bureaucratic formalization generated by succession in management is not inevitable; collective resistance can arrest it.

The miners, so to speak, had evolved an unofficial bureaucratic apparatus of their own. Their effective informal
organization, by regulating their work, took the place of
a more formal system of control and simultaneously gave
them sufficient power to defeat endeavors to impose a
formal system of discipline upon them against their will.
Did efficiency suffer? Gouldner implies it did not, although

he does not specifically deal with this question. In any case, the conduct of the miners calls attention, once more, to the importance of informal relations and unofficial practices in bureaucratic structures, which is the topic of the next chapter.

Bureaucracy in Process

A BUREAUCRACY in operation appears quite different from the abstract portrayal of its formal structure. Many official rules are honored in the breach; the members of the organization act as human beings—often friendly and sometimes annoyed—rather than like dehumanized impersonal machines.

But this contradiction between official requirements and actual conduct in bureaucracies may be more apparent than real. Perhaps the violation of some rules is inconsequential for the organization and the essential regulations are regularly obeyed. It is also possible that a detached attitude is required only in those relationships that are involved in the transaction of official business, such as employee-client or subordinate-superior, and congenial informality is confined to relationships between employees who work next to one another but not with one another, such as the members of a stenographic pool. However, even if such clear-cut divisions between formal and informal spheres were always to exist, and this is by no means the case, it would still be relevant to inquire whether informal relations and unofficial practices have any significant effects on operations and the achievement of organizational objectives. This is the task of the present chapter.

Bureaucracy's Other Face

Cases from three different kinds of organization have been selected for presentation. They deal, respectively, with a military, an industrial, and a civil-service bureaucracy. All of them reveal "bureaucracy's other face," as Charles H. Page calls the unofficial activities and interactions that are so prominent in the daily operations of formal organizations. These concrete cases furnish the basis for a reexamination of the concept of bureaucratic organization and its relation to administrative efficiency.

In the Navy

The existence and importance of the informal structure of the Navy would hardly be denied by any experienced participant . . . Like the formal, it consists of rules, groupings, and sanctioned systems of procedure. They are informal because they are never recorded in the codes or official blueprints and because they are generated and maintained with a degree of spontaneity always lacking in the activities which make up the formal structure. These rules, groupings, and procedures do, nevertheless, form a structure, for, though not *officially* recognized, they are clearly and semipermanently established, they are just as "real" and just as compelling on the membership as the elements of the official structure, and they maintain their existence and social significance throughout many changes of personnel. . . .

[The newcomer] has two large segments of Navy organization to learn. The high-pressure instruction of the indoctrination school or boot camp, the Navy teacher and his own study of the documents can reveal the intricacies of the Navy's formal structure. . . . But knowledge of the informal structure, which is at least as necessary for successful participation, must be gained through experience in the group itself. . . .

Many pressing problems develop within the Navy, *efficient* solutions for which are not possible within the framework of the official institutional structure. . . . Such a problem is the constant and, to the initiated, conspicuous one of official communication between officers. Official communications in most cases must, according to regulations, be routed through the "chain of command" for whatever endorsements the officers in the chain judge appropriate. . . . Yet very frequently the circumvention of this regulation appears as precisely the solution of a pressing problem. When such a development occurs the individuals involved, if they are sophisticated in the ways of their organization, will operate on the level of the informal structure wherein a solution is usually possible, and will thereby avoid that bureaucratic frustration so frequently felt by those who are strict followers of "the book." . . . .

One extreme example, an island air base whose position and absence of native population guaranteed almost no contact with extra-Navy persons, had experienced a major structural change from the time it had been based in the United States. In this case the informal structure had almost altogether lost its private sanctification and stood, in large measure, as the officially recognized pattern of this group of temporary island residents. One visiting officer described this as a "breakdown" of the organization. This was clearly not the case, as shown by the high morale and the effective accomplishment of missions. What had "broken down" was a large part of the formal structure, or rather it had been submerged as the informal structure rose into overt recognition and use. Fortunately the "skipper" as well as several other officers and petty officers were "natural leaders": their status and role definitions were somewhat parallel in the two structures. However, unmistakable indications of the superordination of the informal included the replacement of the social isolation of the commanding officer by his very keen participation in all activities of the unit, the submergence of the rejected types whatever their rank or rate to the informally defined roles, the emergence of the natural leaders to what amounted to official recognition, the abandonment of most of the officially governing protocol (except in the treatment of visitors), and accomplishment of the day-to-day and long-run tasks with efficiency, zeal, and spontaneous initiative not characteristic of official bureaucratic machinery.[1]

In a Factory

Of the fourteen men, or operators, as they were called in the Western Electric Company, who were regularly in the Observation Room, nine were wiremen, . . . three were soldermen, . . . and two were inspectors. . . . The men were engaged in making parts of switches for central office telephone equipment. Specifically, they were connecting wires to banks of terminals. . . . A wireman took the necessary number of banks for an equipment and placed them in a holder or fixture on a workbench. Then he connected the terminals of the banks together in a certain order with wire. . . . A wireman worked on two equipments at a time. Having finished a level on one equipment, he moved to the second equipment. In the meantime, a solderman fixed in place the finished connections of the first equipment, and an inspector tested and scrutinized the work of both men. . . .

Let us now turn to some of the activities, over and above each man's special job, that were observed in the room. One of the commonest was helping another man out by doing some of his wiring for him when he had fallen behind. Although no formal rule of the company said that one man should not help another, helping was in practice forbidden, on the theory that the jobs were one-man jobs and that each man could do his own best. Nevertheless a good deal of help was given. The wiremen said it made them feel good to be helped. . . . Everyone took part in helping. Unlike some other activities, it was not confined to one social group. . . .

In the lunch hour and from time to time during the work, the men in the room took part in all sorts of games. Almost anything was an excuse for a bet: matching coins, lagging coins, shooting craps, cards, combinations of digits in the serial numbers of weekly pay checks. Pools were organized on horse racing, baseball, and quality records. . . . Participation in games occurred for the most part within two groups . . . , a group at the front of the room . . . [and] a group at the back. . . . The material collected by the observer could also be interpreted to show that friendships or antagonisms existed between certain men in the room. . . . Except for a friendship between [two men], all friendships occurred within one or the other of the two groups already mapped out on the basis of participation in games. . . .

Roethlisberger and Dickson sum up all this evidence by saying that, although the members of the Bank Wiring Observation Room were pulled together in some ways, for instance, in mutual help and in restriction of output, in others they were divided. In particular, there were two cliques in the room, whose membership was approximately that revealed by participation in games. . . . [But three men] were in no sense members of either clique, [two of them] attracting much antagonism. Each clique had its own games and activities, noticeably different from those of the other group. . . .

If, as we have seen, the output rates of the wiremen

could not be correlated with their intelligence or dexterity, they could clearly be correlated with clique membership. . . . [The members of one clique] had the
lowest output.[2]

In a Federal Law-Enforcement Agency

The principal duties of agents were carried out in the
field. Cases of firms to be investigated were assigned to
them individually by the supervisor. Processing a case
involved an audit of the books and records of the firm,
interviews with the employer (or his representative)
and a sample of employees, the determination of the
existence of legal violation and the appropriate action
to be taken, and negotiations with employers. . . . If
an agent encountered a problem he could not solve, he
was expected to consult his supervisor, who, if he could
not furnish the requested advice himself, gave the agent
permission to consult a staff attorney. Agents were not
allowed to consult anyone else directly, not even their
colleagues. . . .

Agents, however, were reluctant to reveal to their
supervisor their inability to solve a problem for fear
that their ratings would be adversely affected. . . .
Their need for getting advice without exposing their
difficulties to the supervisor constrained agents to consult one another, in violation of the official rule. . . .

A consultation can be considered an exchange of
values; both participants gain something, and both have
to pay a price. The questioning agent is enabled to perform better than he could otherwise have done, without
exposing his difficulties to the supervisor. By asking for
advice, he implicitly pays his respect to the superior
proficiency of his colleague. This acknowledgement of
inferiority is the cost of receiving assistance. The consultant gains prestige, in return for which he is willing
to devote some time to the consultation and permit it to
disrupt his own work. The following remark of an agent
illustrates this: "I like giving advice. It's flattering, I

suppose, if you feel that the others come to you for advice."

The expert whose advice was often sought by colleagues obtained social evidence of his superior abilities. This increased his confidence in his own decisions, and thus improved his performance as an investigator. . . . The role of the agent who frequently solicited advice was less enviable, even though he benefited most directly from this unofficial practice. Asking a colleague for guidance was less threatening than asking the supervisor, but the repeated admission of his inability to solve his own problems also undermined the self-confidence of an agent and his standing in the group. The cost of advice became prohibitive if the consultant, after the questioner had subordinated himself by asking for help, was in the least discouraging—by postponing a discussion or by revealing his impatience during one. To avoid such rejections, agents usually consulted a colleague with whom they were friendly, even if he was not an expert. . . .

An agent who worked on an interesting case and encountered strange problems often told his fellow agents about it. . . . These presentations of complex cases assisted the speaker in solving his problems. They were consultations in disguise. . . . The agent who attempted to arrive at decisions while sitting alone at his desk defined the situation as preparing the case for submission to the supervisor. His anxiety, engendered by the supervisor's evaluation of his decisions, interfered most with clear thinking in this situation. Instead of trying to make important official decisions, an agent could discuss the interesting aspects of his case with one of his colleagues. This situation, defined as a discussion among friends, did not evoke anxiety. On the contrary, it destroyed the anxiety which pervaded the decision-making process.

The listener was not merely a friend but a fellow specialist in solving the problems which occurred in investigations. This created the possibility of interruption, if the suggested interpretation required correction. A listener might remind the speaker that he forgot to take some factor into account, or that the data lend themselves to alternative conclusions. The assent implicit in the absence of interruptions and in attentive listening destroyed the doubts that continuously arose in the process of making many minor decisions in order to arrive at a conclusion. The admiration for the clever solution of the problem advanced, expressed by interested questions and appreciative comments, increased the speaker's confidence in his partial solutions while groping for the final one. By reducing his anxiety, "thinking out loud" enabled an official to associate relevant pieces of information and pertinent regulations, and thus to arrive at decisions of which he might not have thought while alone. . . .

[This pattern of explicit and disguised consultations] transformed an aggregate of individuals who happened to have the same supervisor into a cohesive group. The recurrent experience of being dependent on the group, whose members furnished needed help, and of being appreciated by the others in the group, as indicated by their solicitations for assistance, created strong mutual bonds. . . . Second, this practice contributed to operating efficiency, because it improved the quality of the decisions of agents. Every agent knew that he could obtain help with solving problems whenever he needed it. This knowledge, reinforced by the feeling of being an integrated member of a cohesive group, decreased anxiety about making decisions. Simultaneously, being often approached for advice raised the self-confidence of an investigator. The very existence of this practice enhanced the ability of all agents, experts as well as others, to make decisions independently.[3]

Organization of Work Groups

When we examine sufficiently small segments of bureaucracies to observe their operations in detail, we discover patterns of activities and interactions that cannot be accounted for by the official structure. Whether the work group is part of the armed forces, a factory, or civilian government, it is characterized by a network of informal relations and a set of unofficial practices which have been called its "informal organization." This concept calls attention to the fact that deviations from the formal blueprint are socially organized patterns and not merely the consequence of fortuitous personality differences. Helping others or playing games was the established practice in the Bank Wiring Observation Room, not a manifestation of the rebellious personality of one or the other individual. Variations in productivity were not due to the fact that the mechanical ability of some workers happened to be superior to that of others but to the social organization of the group, as indicated by the finding that productivity was related to clique membership and not to manual dexterity or intelligence.

Regularities do not occur accidentally. That official rules bring them about is expected, but what is the source of those regularities in social conduct that do not reflect official standards? They are also the result of normative standards, but standards that have emerged in the work group itself rather than having been officially instituted by superiors or formal blueprints. In the course of social interaction at work, there arise patterned expectations and norms, which find expression in a network of social relationships and in prevailing practices. As each worker in the Bank Wiring Observation Room grew accustomed to playing games with some coworkers and not with others, his role became socially defined as part of one of the two cliques, or of neither, and the group became structured accordingly. Simultaneously, there developed normative beliefs shared by all members of the group: "Don't be a rate-buster by working too fast!" "Don't be a chiseler by working too slowly!" "Don't act bossy!" "Don't be a squealer!" These unofficial standards governed the behavior of the workers. One inspector was excluded from both cliques, because he acted officiously and even reported other workers to superiors. Despite a complicated wage incentive system, there existed some restriction of output. Since too fast as well as too slow work was condemned, wiremen did not try to produce as much as they could, although doing so would have increased their pay, but slacked their pace after they had completed what they considered to be "a fair day's work." Differences in output within this group would probably have been smaller if it had not been divided into two cliques. One of these emphasized that the worker should not produce too much, and the other, that he should not produce too little, so that the members of each clique enjoyed social support for working slower or faster, respectively, than those of the other.

To be effective, social norms must be enforceable. Unless a member of a formal organization conforms with its official regulations to a certain minimum degree, he will be expelled. The reverse of this statement is also true: unless expulsion is a serious threat, the prevalence of conformity cannot be assured. The individual's motivation to remain part of the organization makes him subject to its control. Salaried employees are more dependable than unpaid volunteers in large part because economic dependence is a reliable mechanism for interesting the members of the organization in keeping their positions. The same principle holds for the enforcement of unofficial norms. Whereas the work group does not have the power to remove one of its members from his job and deprive him of his income, it can ostracize him and thereby exclude him from genuine group membership. But for such exclusion to be a threat that discourages deviant tendencies, the individual must first wish to be included in the group. If a person did not care about maintaining congenial relations with his coworkers, being cold-shouldered by them would neither disconcert him nor deter him from disregarding their social norms; and for him it would be "their" norms rather than "ours."

This is the reason why the existence of social cohesion is so significant for work groups. Strong mutual ties between the members of a group make each interested in maintaining his position in the group. In this situation, unofficial norms can readily be enforced, and it is rarely necessary to resort to the extreme penalty of ostracism, since lesser sanctions suffice to sustain conformity. If an individual violates a norm highly valued by the other members of the group, they will become less friendly toward him; this is virtually an automatic reaction when somebody's behavior displeases us. Such a change in interpersonal relationships endangers the individual's standing in the group and induces him, if he is identified with the group, to refrain from similar violations in the future in order to regain the favor of his colleagues or, at least, to prevent his relations with them from deteriorating further. Another type of informal sanction can be termed "ostracism in miniature." When several members of a group together ridicule a colleague or express aggression against him in some other form because he has violated an unofficial norm, they furnish him with a brief but concentrated demonstration of the nature of ostracism by standing united in opposition to him alone. The extremely disagreeable experience of feeling isolated while witnessing the solidarity of others constitutes a powerful incentive to abandon deviant practices lest this temporary state become a permanent one.

The effective enforcement of unofficial standards of conduct in cohesive work groups has important implications for official operations. Many studies have found that the existence of cohesive bonds between coworkers is a prerequisite for high morale and optimum performance of duties,[4] but this does not mean that all norms that arise in cohesive work groups contribute to the accomplishment of official tasks. The group's own standards in the Bank Wiring Observation Room, for example, since they discouraged the fastest workers from producing at a maximum rate, lowered productivity (although these standards simultaneously encouraged the slowest workers to increase their output). On the other hand, the fact that an unofficial practice directly conflicts with official regulations does not necessarily signify that it is detrimental to operating efficiency. The practice of consulting colleagues in violation of an official rule in the government agency apparently improved efficiency in operations, and so did the informal patterns on the island air base that defied the Navy's formal codes.

Paradoxically, unofficial practices that are explicitly prohibited by official regulations sometimes further the achievement of organizational objectives. This crucial finding raises questions about the concept of "informal organization" and about bureaucratic efficiency. Social scientists often set up a dichotomy between the informal and the formal organization and attempt to place every observation into one of these pigeonholes. This procedure can only be misleading, since the distinction is an analytical one: there is only one actual organization. When government agents make official decisions in the course of informal discussions, their conduct cannot meaningfully be classified as belonging to either the formal or the informal organization. Even when a factory employee worked more slowly than he otherwise might have in conformity with unofficial norms, his behavior was also influenced by the formal requirements to manufacture telephone equipment and to use certain production methods for this purpose. Official as well as unofficial standards, formal as well as informal social relations, affect the ways in which the daily operations in work groups become organized, but the result is *one* social organization in each work group, not two.

Other problems posed by the finding that operating efficiency is sometimes increased by violating the very rules designed to maximize efficiency call for a more detailed discussion.

Bureaucracy's New Face

Bureaucracies are not such rigid structures as is popularly assumed. Their organization does not remain fixed according to the formal blueprint, but always evolves into new forms. Conditions change, problems arise, and, in the course of coping with them, the members of the organization establish new procedures and often transform their social relationships, thereby modifying the structure. The organized patterns of activities and interactions that have not—perhaps, not yet—been officially institutionalized reveal bureaucracy in the process of change.

Some of the practices that emerge in the course of operations further the attainment of organizational objectives, while others hinder it. The official interest of the bureaucratic organization demands that the latter development be discouraged and the former encouraged. The administrative problem is how to bring this about.

Irrationality of Rationalistic Administration   "Scientific management" has attempted to rationalize industrial production and administration by discovering and applying the most efficient methods of operations.[5] Time-and-motion studies are a well-known illustration of this approach: the motions required by the most skilled workers for performing a given task in the shortest possible time are determined, and these exact motions are taught to other workers. But, as one writer points out, "managerial technologists have been far more successful in demonstrating efficient procedures for maximum productivity than they have been in getting such procedures accepted by workers." [6] This failure of scientific management was the inevitable result of its assumption, most evident in "scientific" wage incentive systems, that rational economic interests alone govern the conduct of employees and of its neglect of social factors. To administer a social organization according to purely technical criteria of rationality is irrational, because it ignores the nonrational aspects of social conduct.

From an abstract standpoint, the most rational method of effecting uniformity and coordination in a large organization would appear to be to devise efficient procedures for every task and insist that they be strictly followed. In practice, however, such a system would not function effectively for several reasons. One is that it implicitly assumes that management is omniscient. No system of rules and supervision can be so finely spun that it anticipates all exigencies that may arise. Changes in external conditions create new administrative problems, and the very innovations introduced to solve them often have unanticipated consequences that produce further problems. For example, the interviewers in a public employment agency were evaluated on the basis of the number of applicants for jobs they interviewed per month. As jobs became scarce after World War II, interviewers, induced by this method of evaluation to work fast, tended to dismiss clients for whom jobs could not be located quickly. In the interest of effective employment service, it was necessary to discourage such tendencies. For this purpose, a new method of evaluation, based primarily on the number of applicants placed in jobs, was instituted. This innovation did motivate interviewers to exert greater efforts to find jobs for clients, but it also gave rise to competition for the slips on which job openings were recorded, which interviewers sometimes even hid from one another, and these competitive practices were a new obstacle to efficient operations. In response to this emergent problem, the most cohesive group of interviewers developed cooperative norms and successfully suppressed competitive tendencies, with the result that productive efficiency increased.[7] Unless the members of the organization have the freedom and initiative to deal with operating problems as they come up, efficiency will suffer.

Moreover, some impediments to operating efficiency cannot be eradicated by official decree. This is the case with respect to the anxieties and feelings of *anomie* (a state of feeling isolated and disoriented) that often arise among the lower echelons of bureaucratic hierarchies. Informal relations in cohesive work groups reduce such disruptive tensions. But once cohesive groups exist in the bureaucracy, as we have seen, they will develop their own standards of conduct and enforce them among their members. Administrative efficiency cannot be served by ignoring the fact that the performance of individuals is affected by their relations with colleagues, but only by taking cognizance of this fact and attempting to create those conditions in the organization that lead to unofficial practices which further rather than hinder the achievement of its objectives.

Finally, in a democratic culture, where independence of

action and equality of status are highly valued, detailed
rules and close supervision are resented, and resentful
employees are poorly motivated to perform their duties
faithfully and energetically. A striking contrast exists
between the rigorous discipline employees willingly impose
upon themselves, because they realize that their work
requires strict operating standards, and the constant annoyance at being hamstrung by picayune rules that they
experience as arbitrarily imposed upon them. The members
of the federal agency, for instance, often objected to
having to fill out forms precisely, as we all do, and to
other minor internal rules, but they freely accepted the
much more stringent discipline of adhering strictly to legal
regulations in their investigations, which was necessitated
by law enforcement itself. To repress the ability for self-
imposed discipline and to undermine the motivation to
exert efforts by prescribing in detail how every task is to
be performed is wasteful, to say the least. A more efficient
method of bureaucratic administration is to channel this
ability and motivation to serve the ends of the organization.

These considerations suggest a revision of the concept
of bureaucratic structure. Rather than considering it an
administrative system with particular characteristics, it
may be preferable to follow another lead of Weber's and
to conceive of bureaucracy in terms of its purpose. Bureaucracy, then, can be defined as organization that maxi-
mizes efficiency in administration, whatever its formal
characteristics, or as an institutionalized method of organizing social conduct in the interest of administrative
efficiency. On the basis of this definition, the problem of
central concern is the expeditious removal of the obstacles
to efficient operations which recurrently arise. This cannot
be accomplished by a preconceived system of rigid procedures, as the preceding discussion suggests, but only by

creating conditions favorable to continuous adjustive development in the organization. To establish such a pattern of self-adjustment in a bureaucracy, conditions must prevail that encourage its members to cope with emergent problems and to find the best method for producing specified results on their own initiative, and that obviate the need for unofficial practices which thwart the objectives of the organization, such as restriction of output.

What are these conditions? We do not have sufficient empirical evidence to give a conclusive answer to this question. But some tentative hypotheses can be advanced, although these must be qualified by the recognition that the same conditions may not be required for adjustive development in other cultures or in other historical periods.

Conditions of Adjustive Development

1. *Employment security*   For the members of an organization to assume responsibility for finding new ways of solving problems, they must have some employment security. It is often held that only the danger of losing one's job stimulates initiative and that security kills it, but this view seems to be fallacious. Say that your job would not be affected one way or the other, would you, personally, rather follow simple routines or assume challenging responsibilities in your work? Most people prefer the latter and will exercise initiative if they are given a chance. The insecurity engendered by the knowledge that his job hangs in the balance, however, constrains the employee to adhere closely to familiar and officially sanctioned procedures and to avoid taking risks. It therefore destroys his initiative, since taking the initiative always involves the risk of possible failure.

The situation in the employment agency referred to above illustrates this principle. When a new evaluation system was introduced, it will be remembered, competitive

conflicts were effectively eliminated in one group but
persisted in another. A main reason for this difference was
that the interviewers in the first group held secure civil
service positions, whereas most interviewers in the second
group did not; they were on probation pending permanent
appointment at that time, because only temporary appoint-
ments had been made during the war. The insecure members of the latter group were so anxious to comply with
official demands that they dared not initiate cooperative
practices on their own. The secure members of the former
group, in contrast, felt free to institute cooperative practices, which resulted in higher productivity. Insecurity
generates rigidity and resistance to change, as will be
shown at greater length in Chapter Five.

2. *Internalized standards of workmanship* Employees
must feel free to exercise initiative, but they must also feel
constrained by strict operating principles in doing so, lest
their spontaneous actions interfere with the attainment of
organizational objectives. External restraints, such as detailed rules of operations, are not well suited for this
purpose, since they tend to eliminate discretion completely. If a person, on the other hand, has fully internalized rigorous standards of workmanship, he can exercise his
ingenuity while remaining guided by them; indeed, he finds
gratification in doing precisely that. This is true of the sur-
geon, who applies his talent in new ways in virtually every
operation without deviating from exacting medical standards; of the scientist, whose search for new explanations is
governed by disciplined scientific methods; of the artist,
the expert mechanic, and, as a matter of fact, of every
skilled craftsman who is interested in competent performance of tasks in accordance with abstract principles commonly agreed upon among the members of the occupational group. Identification with abstract standards of
performance permits disciplined discretion in finding new

solutions to problems that conform with these standards. Furthermore, it makes this course of action intrinsically satisfying and thus supplies strong incentives for exerting efforts in one's work.

The prevalence of such a workmanlike or professional orientation among the members of an organization depends in part on certain employment and working conditions. Personnel policies must insure, as they usually do in bureaucracies, that only employees with adequate training and technical qualifications are hired, and that their careers are relatively secure. In addition, however, employees must be made responsible for the performance of challenging tasks, not obligated to follow rigid routines, and they, collectively, must have a voice in the determination of the standards of workmanship that govern their work. It can hardly be an accident that the emergence of such standards has been most pronounced among independent professionals and free artisans. The occupational group that develops its own discipline can most readily enforce it. Finally, it is unlikely that this type of orientation will be characteristic of most workers in industrial concerns and white-collar offices until technological progress has eliminated the most routine tasks, which cannot be expected to arouse a pride of workmanship.

3. *Cohesive work groups.* The dilettante, who has no definite responsibilities, and the human robot, whose duties are rigidly fixed, have, for opposite reasons, no cause for anxiety. But responsibility for the effective performance of complex tasks tends to engender anxiety. In the federal agency of law enforcement, for example, officials were held responsible for making accurate decisions in difficult investigations, which required ingenuity, since the diversity of situations prevented strict adherence to exact rules. Their freedom to exercise initiative in the process of arriving at correct conclusions made their job interesting, but

it also evoked anxieties over decision-making, which interfered with clear thinking and effective operations. As in this case, integrative interaction in cohesive work groups generally relieves disruptive anxieties and tensions and often leads to common new practices that contribute to operating efficiency.

Although social cohesion, another prerequisite of recurrent self-adjustment in the organization, cannot be officially created, conditions favorable for its development can be. Low turn-over of personnel and infrequent transfers within the organization establish the stability of membership conducive to the formation of mutual ties in work groups. In the absence of explicit personnel policies, however, employees may expect to be dismissed or promoted at any time, and hence they are apt to worry about their careers and to feel the need to impress their superiors at all costs. This need is likely to lead to competitive rivalry, which destroys cohesiveness. When promotions and necessary dismissals depend on explicit and openly announced standards, on the other hand, employees are able to predict their career chances with relative accuracy. Most of them, if not all, know that they will not be dismissed except for specified misconduct, and whether there is any likelihood of their being promoted in the near future, as well as the technical criteria that govern advancement. Employees secure in this knowledge have little inclination to endanger their informal relations with colleagues through competitive practices. Explicit personnel policies, which are being adopted by an increasing number of private as well as public bureaucracies, therefore promote social cohesion.

4. *Split in managerial authority*   Cohesiveness empowers work groups to institute common adjustive practices, but these will not advance the organization's objectives if em-

ployees feel that their interest conflicts with that of management. Restriction of output among factory workers, for example, is designed to protect their economic interest against management by reducing the chances of being laid off. (The study of the Western Electric Company was conducted during the depression of the 1930s, when the danger of layoffs due to lack of work was very great indeed.) If employees fear that optimum performance will put some of them out of their jobs, their collective endeavors will hinder rather than further it, since the dominant concern with earning a livelihood will in all likelihood override pride of workmanship. The basic source of this fear is the conflict between the employer's interest in reducing cost and that of employees in their income. This is a real conflict of interest, which cannot be talked out of existence by good labor-management relations, and which would probably persist even in a socialist economy; but its detrimental effects on operations can be avoided, this writer believes, by a split in managerial authority.

Such a split in authority exists in civil service. Management in government agencies, in contrast to management in private industry, controls only operations and not employment conditions. Salaries and the procedures that govern promotion and discharge are determined by civil-service commissions in accordance with legal statutes. Individual government officials, just as private employees, occasionally come into conflict with management in the course of operations. The conflict between the collective economic interest of operating officials and the budgetary considerations of their employer, however, finds expression in their opposition to the civil-service commission and the legislature, which set the conditions of their employment. This conflict does not harm their relationship with the agency's administration. On the contrary, operating officials and administrators are united by a common interest in legislation that benefits civil servants. Employees who have no reason to protect their economic welfare against the management of their own organization are more apt to maintain a professional or workmanlike concern with perfecting methods of operations and thus to contribute to continuous adjustive development in the organization.

5. *Evaluation on the basis of clearly specified results* The standardization required for uniform and coordinated performance would seem to preclude the exercise of initiative which has been so much emphasized in the preceding discussion. To be sure, this is the case when operating procedures are standardized in minute detail, but there is no need for such close regulations unless the members of the organization are not qualified to perform responsible tasks. If they are qualified, it is probably enough to standardize the end-products of their operations and not the precise ways they arrive at them. Evaluation on the basis of clearly specified results, which employees are expected to accomplish in their work, encourages ingenuity and simultaneously assures the standardization necessary for effective bureaucratic operation.

The Task of the Administrator   These five conditions and, at least, one other, which will be discussed in the following chapter, characterize *bureaucracy's new face*. Once they are met, needed adjustments occur quite spontaneously, as it were, within the organization. This self-adjustment largely relieves the administrator of the duty of coping with emergent operating problems himself, giving him more time for discharging other responsibilities. Bureaucratic processes continually endanger the conditions for optimum performance; necessary reductions in staff give rise to feelings of insecurity despite explicit personnel policies; the anxieties engendered by evaluation on the basis of results may not be relieved by social cohesion; and so forth. The main task of the new administrator is to keep vigilant watch over these conditions of adjustive development, which are perpetually threatened, but without which, if the hypotheses advanced here are correct, efficiency in the bureaucracy suffers.

4

Bureaucratic Authority

THE HIERARCHY of authority in a bureaucracy, essential
for coordination, often produces among its lower echelons
profound feelings of inequality and apathy that impede
identification with the organization's objectives. The initia-
tion of needed adjustments by the operating members of
the organization presupposes, in addition to the five conditions already discussed, a method of hierarchical coordination that minimizes these harmful consequences for
work motivation. After analyzing the ways in which
bureaucratic authority is exercised, we shall return to this
problem at the end of this chapter.

To start with, let us consider another paradox between
official requirements and actual practice. In theory, bureaucratic superiors are expected to exert strict and impersonal control over subordinates. But in fact, immediate
supervisors and foremen frequently "play ball" with their

subordinates and let them "get away with" infractions of many rules. What accounts for this leniency?

Strategic Leniency and Authority

A psychological explanation of the failure to enforce strict discipline among subordinates might attribute it to poor leadership. Some supervisors are overly lenient, it could be held, because inborn or acquired personality traits prevent them from asserting their authority over others and maintaining effective leadership. Note that this explanation assumes as a matter of course that the bureaucratic superior who appears lenient merely indulges his subordinates and is less effective than the disciplinarian in discharging his supervisory responsibilities. Empirical evidence, however, indicates that the very opposite is the case.

A study of twenty-four clerical sections in an insurance company analyzed the relationship between method of supervision and productive efficiency.[1] In closely supervised sections, whose heads gave clerks detailed instructions and frequently checked up on them, productivity was usually lower than in sections where employees were given more freedom to do the work in their own way. Moreover, supervisors who were primarily concerned with maintaining a high level of production, interestingly enough, were less successful in meeting this goal than those supervisors who were more interested in the welfare of their subordinates than in sheer production; in the latter case, productivity was generally higher. Finally, groups who worked under more authoritarian supervisors were, on the whole, less productive than those supervised in a relatively democratic fashion. Other studies have also found that disciplinarian supervisors are less effective than more liberal ones.[2]

Such findings are often misinterpreted as signifying that

democratic ways are superior to authoritarian ones. But this is a rather loose use of the term "democratic," the exact meaning of which is worth preserving. Since "democracy" denotes rule from below (literally, "people's rule") and not from above, one person's supervision of others can, by definition, not be democratic. This is not the place for a discussion of the relation between democracy and bureaucracy; the final chapter is reserved for this purpose. But here it should be noted that tolerant supervisory practices, in contrast to disciplinarian ones, are neither democratic nor an indication that controlling power over subordinates has been surrendered. On the contrary, leniency in supervision is a potent strategy, consciously or unconsciously employed, for establishing authority over subordinates, and this is why the liberal supervisor is particularly effective.

Let us clarify the concept of authority. First, it refers to a relationship between persons and not to an attribute of one individual. Second, authority involves exercise of social control which rests on the *willing* compliance of subordinates with certain directives of the superior. He need not coerce or persuade subordinates in order to influence them, because they have accepted as legitimate the principle that some of their actions should be governed by his decisions. Third, authority is an observable pattern of interaction and not an official definition of a social relationship. If a mutinous crew refuses to obey the captain's orders, he does not in fact have authority over his men. Whatever the superior's official rights to command obedience and the subordinates' official duties to obey him, his authority over them extends only to conduct that they voluntarily permit to be governed by his directives. Actual authority, consequently, is not granted by the formal organizational chart, but must be established in the course of social interaction, although the official bu-

reaucratic structure, as we shall see presently, facilitates its
establishment.

What are some of the practices of a lenient foreman
or supervisor? Above all, he allows subordinates to violate
minor rules, to smoke or talk, for example, despite the
fact that it is prohibited by management. This permissive-
ness often increases his power over them by furnishing
him with legitimate sanctions that he can use as he sees fit.
If an action of his subordinates displeases him, the super-
viser can punish them by commanding: "Cut out the
smoking! Can't you read the sign?" Had he always enforced the rule, this penalty would not have been available
to him. Indeed, so crude a use of sanctions is rarely necessary. The mere knowledge that the rule exists and, possibly, that it is enforced elsewhere, instills a sense of obliga-
tion to liberal superiors and induces subordinates more
readily to comply with their requests.

Whereas the disciplinarian supervisor generally asserts
his official prerogatives, the lenient and relaxed one does
not. The latter attempts to take the wishes of his subordinates into account in arranging their work schedule, although he has the right to assign their work at his own
discretion. Sometimes he goes to special trouble to ac-
commodate a subordinate. Instead of issuing curt commands, he usually explains the reasons for his directives.
He calls his subordinates by their first names and encourages their use of his first name (especially in democratically minded American organizations). When one of
his subordinates gets into difficulties with management,
he is apt to speak up for him and to defend him. These
different actions have two things in common: the superior
is not required to do them, and his subordinates greatly
welcome his doing them. Such conduct therefore creates
social obligations. To repay the supervisor for past favors,
and not to risk the cessation of similar favors in the fu-

ture, subordinates voluntarily comply with many of his requests, including some they are not officially required to obey. By refraining from exercising his power of control whenever it is legitimate to do so, the bureaucratic superior establishes effective authority over subordinates, which enables him to control them much more effectively than otherwise would be possible.

Complementary role expectations arise in the course of interaction between superior and subordinates and become crystallized in the course of interaction among subordinates. As the superior permits subordinates to violate some rules and to make certain decisions themselves, and as they grow accustomed to conform with many of his directives, they learn to expect to exercise discretion in some areas and to follow supervisory directives in others, and he learns to expect this pattern of conduct from them. The members of the work group, by watching one another at work and talking among themselves about the manner in which they perform their duties, develop social consensus about these role expectations and thereby reinforce them. The newcomer to the group, who must be taught "how things are done around here" as distinguished from "what's in the book," provides an opportunity for further affirming this consensus by making it explicit.

The resulting common role expectations are often so fully internalized that employees are hardly aware of being governed by them. The members of one department might find it natural for their supervisor to interrupt their work and tell them to start on a new task. The members of another department in the same organization might consider such a supervisory order as gross interference with their work, since they had become accustomed to using their discretion about the sequence of their tasks, yet readily comply with other directives of the supervision. These role expectations of independence from the supervisor in some areas and unquestioning obedience in others define the limits of his authority over subordinates.

Power of Sanction

The preceding comments apply to informal leadership as well as to bureaucratic authority. The informal leader, like the prudent bureaucratic superior, establishes his authority over his followers by creating social obligations.[3] Once a relationship of authority exists, both bureaucratic superior and informal leader can afford to word their orders as mere suggestions, because even these are readily followed by the rest of the group. Neither of them usually needs sanctions to command obedience, though sanctions are available to both of them in case they wish to use special inducements, since praise or blame of the person in the superordinate position itself exerts a powerful influence.

Nevertheless, there is a fundamental distinction between informal leadership and bureaucratic authority. Informal leadership freely emerges among a group of peers. It is initially the result of personality differences that have become socially magnified. Some members of the group excel in activities that are highly valued by all, whether these are street fighting or solving complex problems; these few will be more respected, and their opinions will carry greater weight. The person in the extreme position, if he also finds ways to obligate the others to him, is expected to be the group's leader.

Bureaucratic authority, on the other hand, prevents the group itself from conferring the position of leadership upon the member of their choice. The voluntary obedience of subordinates must converge upon the individual officially placed in the position of supervisor, irrespective of his personal characteristics. The bureaucratic mechanism that makes this state of affairs a predictable occurrence is the superior's power to impose sanctions, typically in the form of periodic ratings of the performance of his subordinates, which influence their chances of advancement and of keeping their jobs.

The dependency of bureaucratic subordinates upon their immediate superior produced by his rating power engenders frustrations and anxieties for adults. It forces employees to worry about their supervisor's reaction at every step they take. An effective way to weaken or avoid such feelings is to identify with the bureaucratic system of normative standards and objectives. By making this system a part of their own thinking, employees transform conformity with its principles from submission to the superior's demands into voluntary action. Guided by internalized standards, they are less likely to experience external restraints in performing their duties. Moreover, once the hierarchical division of responsibility has been accepted as a basic principle of the organization, it becomes less threatening to a person's self-esteem to obey the supervisor's directives, since he is known to be duty-bound to issue them, just as it is not degrading to obey the traffic directions of a policeman. Dependence on the superior's rating encourages the adoption of a bureaucratic orientation, for the disadvantages of dependence can thereby be evaded.

It is of crucial importance that this process of identification with bureaucratic standards does not occur in isolation but in a social situation. All members of the work group find themselves in the same position of dependence on their supervisor. (In fact, all members of the bureaucratic organization are, in varying degrees, dependent on their immediate superiors.) Together, they can obtain concessions from the supervisor, because he is anxious to obligate them by granting some of their demands. In exchange, they feel constrained to comply with many of his directives. Typically, a strict definition is given to the limits of this effective authority. Subordinates can often be heard to remark: "That's the supervisor's responsibility. He gets paid for making those decisions." This does not mean that operating employees shirk responsibilities, as indicated by their willingness to shoulder those they define as their own. But the social agreement among the members of the work group that making certain decisions and issuing certain directives is the duty of the supervisor, not merely his privilege, serves to emphasize that following them does not constitute submission to his arbitrary will but conformity with commonly accepted operating principles. In such a situation, which prevails in some organizations though by no means in all, subordinates do not experience the supervisor's exercise of authority over them as domination; neither are they necessarily envious of his responsibilities, since they frequently consider their own more challenging than his.

The effective establishment of authority obviates the need for sanctions in daily operations. If a supervisor commands the voluntary obedience of subordinates, he need not induce them to obey him by promising them rewards or threatening them with punishment. In fact, the use of sanctions undermines authority. A supervisor who is in the habit of invoking sanctions to back his orders—"You won't get a good rating unless you do this!"—shows that he does not expect unqualified compliance. As subordinates learn that he does not expect it, they will no longer feel obligated unconditionally to accept his directives. Moreover, employees resent being continually reminded of their dependence on the supervisor by his promises and threats, and such resentment makes them less inclined to carry out his orders.

This is the dilemma of bureaucratic authority: it rests on the power of sanction but is weakened by frequent resort to sanctions in operations. A basic difference, however, should be noted between the periodic rating of the performance of subordinates, which can be called a *diffuse sanction,* and *specific sanctions* recurrently employed to enforce particular commands. Since all employees know that their immediate superior is officially required to evaluate their operations at periodic intervals, this evaluation is neither a sign that he does not expect unqualified compliance with his directives nor a reason for annoyance with him. This diffuse sanction, imposed only annually or every few months, though creating the dependence of subordinates upon their supervisor, does so without constantly endangering their willingness to be guided by his requests, as the habitual use of specific sanctions (including promises of good ratings and threats of poor ones) would.

While the mere fact that the supervisor administers ratings is not resented by his subordinates, low ratings might well antagonize some of them. But bureaucratic mechanisms exist that enable the supervisor to shift the blame for negative sanctions. For example, statistical records of performance, which are kept in many white-collar offices as well as factories, furnish the supervisor with objective evidence with which he can justify low ratings by showing the recipients that the poor quality of their work left him no other choice. Instead of blaming the supervisor for giving them a poor rating, these employees are forced to blame themselves or to attribute the rating to the "statistics," which are often accused, rightly or wrongly, of failing to measure the qualitative aspects of performance.*

His intermediate position in the hierarchy provides the supervisor with another justification mechanism. He can place the responsibility for giving low ratings or instituting

---

* Of course, quantitative records also facilitate the supervisor's task of evaluating operations.

unpopular requirements on his superiors, to whom he is accountable. Oftentimes a supervisor or foreman will tell his subordinates that he does not like certain standards any better than they do but "those brass-hats in the front office" insist on them. In most organizations, one or a few superintendents or assistant managers (or deans) become the scapegoats who are blamed for all negative sanctions and unpopular requirements. Since the attitudes of employees toward these administrators in removed positions is much less relevant for effective operations than their attitudes toward their immediate superior, the displacement of aggression from him to them is in the interest of the organization. Clients or customers can also serve as scapegoats of aggression—the supervisor can blame their demands for instituting procedures that inconvenience employees. And if he joins subordinates in ridiculing clients or customers, a frequent practice in service occupations, the supervisor further reduces antagonism against himself by standing united with the employees against outsiders.

Periodic ratings, then, increase the dependency of the members of a bureaucracy on their superiors but at the same time allow them to escape from disturbing feelings of dependency by internalizing the principles that govern operations. Although the responsibilities the supervisor is required to discharge occasionally arouse the animosity of some subordinates, various mechanisms divert such antagonism from the supervisor to other objects. These two elements of the bureaucratic structure conspire to provide a fertile soil for the establishment of supervisory authority. Together, they permit supervisors to obligate subordinates willingly to follow directives.

Various circumstances, however, can prevent such favorable conditions in the bureaucratic organization. The disciplinarian supervisor may antagonize subordinates, through recurrent use of sanctions and in other ways, and thereby undermine his effective authority over them as well as their motivation to put effort into their work. The lenient supervisor may be so reluctant to displease subordinates that he refrains from evaluating their performance in accordance with rigorous standards, giving all of them high ratings. This practice invalidates the incentive system, which enhances the interest of employees in accomplishing specified results in their operations. The manipulative supervisor may employ devious techniques to conceal from subordinates his attempts to impose his arbitrary will upon them, for example, by frequent and unwarranted utilization of scapegoats. While manipulative techniques have a fair chance of being successful in temporary pair relationships, as between customer and salesman, their chances of success in relatively permanent relationships within a group are very slim. For sooner or later, some member is apt to see through them, and he is not likely to keep this a secret. Once they are discovered, manipulative techniques have a boomerang effect. Employees who realize that their superior tries to manipulate them are prone to suspect all of his statements and generally to resist his efforts to influence their performance.

These and other disruptive tendencies can be observed in hierarchical organizations, but methods of supervision that encourage operating efficiency are also evident. In the absence of a much larger body of information about bureaucracies than we now possess, it is impossible to know which of these opposite conditions is more frequent. Nevertheless, the fact that authority is sometimes effectively exercised without domineering subordinates or lowering their morale, rare as this may be, demonstrates that such a state of affairs is actually possible and not merely a utopian ideal type.

Inequality in Hierarchical Organizations

If we assume that hierarchical authority is a prerequisite for effective coordination in a large organization (and though this is not a conclusively established fact overwhelming evidence points in its direction), its members cannot be fully equal in status and power. In a democracy, however, where status prerogatives are frowned upon, intense feelings of inequality among the lower echelons of a bureaucracy have several effects that are detrimental for operations. They inhibit identification with the organization and its objectives, lessen interest in performing tasks to the best of one's abilities, kill initiative, and reduce the chances that emergent operating problems will be readily met. Unless employees consider themselves partners in a common enterprise rather than tools in the hands of management, they are not prone willingly to assume responsibilities of their own.

Whereas a basic conflict exists between coordination and work motivation in bureaucratic organizations, this does not mean that it cannot possibly be resolved. Social inequality is not an all-or-none proposition: there are variations in kind as well as in degree. The high value a person places upon equality of status does not prevent him from obeying the orders of his physician when he is ill. Submitting to the authority of his physician—or lawyer or any expert—does not violate his integrity. This is the case because he is convinced that the doctor does not arbitrarily impose his will upon him, but that the doctor's orders are governed by rational principles that serve a common interest, namely, curing his illness.[4] When it is socially accepted that the person in authority is guided by rational standards in the pursuit of common ends, unquestioning obedience to his directives, although an undeniable sign of inequality in the relationship, is not experienced as subjugation nor does it engender profound feelings of inequality.

Let us now examine, in contrast, three bureaucratic conditions that definitely create pronounced inequalities. 1. *Close supervision* forces employees continually to submit to the demands of their superior. To be told what to do and to be checked throughout the day are quite a different experience from that involved in being governed by the expectation that one's completed work must meet rigorous standards. The latter situation does not entail being constantly dominated by another person; the former does. 2. *Employment of sanctions* in daily operations recurrently asserts the supervisor's power over the members of the work group and contradicts the assumption that he is merely the first among peers. Promises of rewards have this effect no less than threats of punishment. Performance ratings are another major source of inequality. 3. *Arbitrary power* produces even more extensive differences in social status. If their supervisor regularly makes specified decisions, employees can adjust to the situation by accepting these limits to their discretion. If, on the other hand, he expects them to assume responsibility for deciding certain matters, but from time to time imposes his own decisions in these very matters, no similar adjustment is possible. Through this type of action, the supervisor subjects his subordinates to his arbitrary will; probably he is motivated, though he seldom admits this even to himself, primarily by a desire to impress others with his power over them. For were it necessary for him to make these decisions, he could not permit them to be made most of the time by the subordinates themselves. Arbitrary exercise of power arouses the most intense feelings of inequality.

But bureaucratic authority neither depends on these three conditions nor is inevitably accompanied by them,

as can be briefly shown. In the first place, evaluation on
the basis of standards that specify the results to be accomplished constrains employees to discipline themselves and
renders close supervision as well as detailed rules super-
fluous. Statistical records of performance are particularly
effective as an impersonal mechanism of control.[5] Sec-
ondly, the supervisor who commands the voluntary obedience of his subordinates has little need for sanctions to
enforce his directives. To be sure, his effective authority,
which enables him to discharge his supervisory responsibilities without frequent resort to specific sanctions, ultimately rests on a diffuse sanction, the periodic rating.
However, the tendency to put the blame for low ratings on
objective standards or higher administrative officials is not
simply a manipulative technique. Although the supervisor
exercises judgment in evaluating subordinates, he, just as
they, is presumably guided by exacting standards in arriving at his decisions, and he is held accountable by his
superiors for making correct judgments. If the supervisor
conforms with these principles and strives to give fair ratings, his subordinates, while not becoming his equals in
the bureaucracy, do not find themselves dominated by an
unpredictable power that demolishes their self-respect.
Finally, the exercise of bureaucratic authority is a duty,
not a privilege that can be abrogated at will. In this respect, formal requirements and informal expectations
among work groups are in agreement. Only by overstep-
ping both the official and the unofficial limits of his authority can a superior dominate his subordinates in an
arbitrary manner.

These considerations suggest that the pronounced inequalities that are often found in bureaucratic organizations are not essential for coordination or uniformity. If this
conclusion is correct, one of the main tasks of the administrator is to minimize such disruptive inequalities without,

of course, endangering the hierarchical authority needed for coordination. That this is not an impossible task is indicated by the fact that some bureaucratic superiors have accomplished it. That it is not an easy task is the result of inherent tendencies in hierarchical organizations. Superiors, whose responsibilities require that they have some control over subordinates, are under perennial temptation to utilize their power not only in the interest of the organization but also in their own interest, for instance, to facilitate their own work or to satisfy their need of dominating others. If they yield to this temptation, minor inequalities expand into major ones. To suppress such tendencies is far from simple, and even after they have been suppressed, continued watchfulness is required lest they emerge again. The goal, however, may well be worth the effort, since lesser inequalities promise to find expression in a more highly motivated working force.

5

Bureaucracy and Social Change

IF DISCIPLINE does not suffice for effective bureaucratic operation, flexibility also being necessary, it follows that rigidity is disadvantageous for the organization. Whereas this principle has been stressed throughout the preceding discussion, we have not yet examined carefully the socio-psychological processes involved. Why do some members of large organizations resist any change in procedures while others accept innovations with ease? What are the organizational conditions in bureaucracies that give rise to these opposite tendencies?

This question of internal change is distinct from, though not unrelated to, the problem of external change, that is, bureaucracy's role in changing the society of which it is a part. Bureaucratization has been held to be a revolutionary force, on the one hand, and a potent instrument of reaction that makes it virtually impossible to alter the existing institutional structure, on the other. Again, there appear to be contradictory strains that require exploration.

Who Are the Ritualists?

"The clerks of departments find themselves sooner or later in the condition of a wheel screwed on to a machine; the only variation of their lot is to be more or less oiled." In these words, Balzac describes the lot of the bureaucrat in the novel *The Civil Service*. Students of administration similarly have often called attention to the ritualistic concern with the minutiae of routine and the resulting inefficiency that one often encounters in bureaucracies. An excerpt from a study of the civil service in France illustrates these conditions:

> Every large-scale organization controlled from a single center sooner or later finds it advisable to elaborate systematic routine procedures in the interest of fiscal regularity and operational consistency. Private business corporations are no more immune to this process than are government departments. Nor do routine procedures necessarily slow up staff decisions. On the contrary, if they are properly adapted to the daily problems of the enterprise, they expedite action.
>
> An organization conforming closely to the hierarchical principle, however, faces the constant danger that these routine operations will become sterilizing ends in themselves rather than effective means to desirable ends. When this happens the usual result is an entanglement of "red tape," or as the French are wont to call it, *La paperasserie, mere* routine thereby becoming *bad* routine. Formal instructions issued at the center overwhelm those who have to handle out on the circumference concrete situations unforeseen in their variety. Almost inevitably an adequate delegation of discretion to subordinate officials is missing in such a system and the field

agent stationed on the administrative firing line stands helpless before demands for prompt decision and immediate action. The fact that every case must be "referred" somewhere means a postponement of any decision about it, the more circuitous the course of reference, the greater the delay. . . .

Mr. Ford Madox Ford relates his adventures in trying to trace a postal money order gone astray. When this occurs, the usual course is to take the matter up through official channels, give the postman a big tip, or put the case into the hands of "an adviser of public companies." On this occasion, however, Mr. Ford decided to go directly to the *Direction de la Seine des P. T. T.* on the Boulevard Montparnasse. At two o'clock he was ushered into the Director's office by a smiling charwoman. After a half hour the Director returned from lunch and scrutinized the documents with great care. Following further consultation with an official in a blue uniform, the Director announced that Ford should betake himself to the "Chief Sub-office for the Recovery of Money Orders" on the other side of Paris. There he was directed to Room V on the sixth floor. While he conversed with an attractive young woman for an hour about face powders and the like, her chief examined the papers and asked questions about Ford's war record and family, finally instructing him to return to the Boulevard Montparnasse, this time to Room XVI on the third floor. From there he was sent back to Room XI in the Chief Sub-office; thence to Room IV, Boulevard Montparnasse; next to Room III, Chief Sub-office; and finally to the "open sesame"—Room XIII, on Montparnasse. Although assured there that he would receive his money by the first delivery the following day, it actually arrived seven weeks later, only after a generous tip had been showered upon the postman.[1]

Inefficiency of this sort occurs when the members of an organization become so preoccupied with meticulous application of detailed rules that they lose sight of the very purpose of their action. Certain conditions in bureaucratic structures encourage the development of this ritualistic orientation, as Merton notes:

> Discipline can be effective only if the ideal patterns are buttressed by strong sentiments which entail devotion to one's duties, a keen sense of the limitation of one's authority and competence, and methodical performance of routine activities. The efficacy of social structure depends ultimately upon infusing group participants with appropriate attitudes and sentiments. . . . These sentiments are often more intense than is technically necessary. There is a margin of safety, so to speak, in the pressure exerted by these sentiments upon the bureaucrat to conform to his patterned obligations, in much the same sense that added allowances (precautionary overestimations) are made by the engineer in designing the supports for a bridge. But this very emphasis leads to a transference of the sentiments from the *aims* of the organization onto the particular details of behavior required by the rules. Adherence to the rules, originally conceived as a means, becomes transformed into an end-in-itself; there occurs the familiar process of *displacement of goals* whereby "an instrumental value becomes a terminal value." Discipline, readily interpreted as conformance with regulations, whatever the situation, is seen not as a measure designed for specific purposes but becomes an immediate value in the life-organization of the bureaucrat.[2]

The prevention of arbitrary decisions requires that a high respect for disciplined performance of duties be fostered among the members of a bureaucracy. This emphasis sometimes becomes overpowering, with the result that punctilious adherence to formalized procedures is elevated into the primary objective of bureaucratic activities and displaces their original objectives in the thinking of officials. Compelled by this orientation to find the right rule before making the least commitment, a bureaucrat will refuse to take any action if there is no clearcut precedent or if there is the slightest doubt about whether it is entirely within his official sphere of jurisdiction. The well-known phenomenon of "passing the buck" and other practices that obstruct operations are often expressions of this tendency. In one case, an official in the employment agency previously mentioned postponed deciding on the color of a new set of index cards until he could determine what color they were "supposed" to have, completely ignoring that the only purpose of assigning a color to them was to distinguish them from other sets of cards. Officials who find their security in strict adherence to familiar routines, moreover, strongly resist changes in the organization and are incapacitated by new problems that confront them. Rigidities are dysfunctional for operating efficiency even under stable conditions and particularly when emergent problems call for a reorganization of working procedures.

Ritualistic displacement of goals, however, is not characteristic of all members of bureaucratic organizations. Many of them, far from deriving satisfaction from constantly following the same routine, find doing so extremely boring. They often express a desire for more variety in their work and for changes that would relieve its monotony. Since even complex tasks become less interesting once they are fully mastered, many employees welcome frequent changes in procedures because these create new problems which recurrently make their work challenging. As one civil servant in the federal agency previously discussed put it: "Lots of us gripe about the fact that they change things all the time. But if I should be completely honest with you, although I also gripe about having to keep on learning new things, I really like it. That's what keeps the job interesting."

Some officials rigidly oppose innovations in the organi-

zation, while others favor them. What are the structural
constraints in bureaucracies that account for these differences? One of them is the nature of the incentive system.
When strict conformity with specific operating rules is the
basis for evaluation, employees are motivated, as a way of
adapting to this situation, to think of bureaucratic procedures as if they were a sacred ritual, and strong resistance
to change in these procedures must be expected. When
employees, on the other hand, are evaluated in terms of
the results accomplished in their operations, they are encouraged to exercise ingenuity and employ diverse methods
in the interest of maximizing specified accomplishments.
But even in the situation where the evaluation system itself does not foster ritualism other conditions in the
bureaucratic structure may do so.

An analysis of instances of extreme rigidity in hierarchical organizations reveals that they are usually associated
with fear of superiors. For example, a group of officials
was once reprimanded by a high administrative official for
having made an incorrect decision in one of their cases.
Thereupon, they applied the rules literally in similar cases
and refrained from exercising any discretion even when it
was clearly called for; afraid of further reprimand, they
attempted to protect themselves against this danger with
overconformity. Bureaucratic superiors cannot generally
censure a subordinate for following official regulations
exactly, regardless of how inefficient or ridiculous such
action may be in a particular case. Hence, feelings of dependency on superiors and anxiety over their reactions
engender ritualistic tendencies.

Rigid adherence to the established routine is a defense
mechanism against feelings of insecurity. In the study of the
federal agency, the attitudes of a group of officials toward
changes in regulations, which occurred frequently, were
ascertained and related to their competence as investiga-

tors. Not one of the more competent half of this group, but most of the less competent half, voiced objections to these recurrent innovations. From a purely rational standpoint, the opposite finding might have been expected: the agent most familiar with existing regulations and most adept in applying them presumably should have been most disturbed when they were superseded by new ones. This reasoning, however, fails to take into consideration the emotional factors that influence conduct. The anxieties generated by the experience that one's knowledge is not always adequate for one's tasks can be calmed by making a ritual of conformity with those procedures with which one has become familiar. Changes in procedures constitute a threat to this method of coping with anxieties and, consequently, must be strenuously resisted. Only in the absence of predominant feelings of insecurity can the desire to escape monotony emerge as a motivating force. Officials who feel secure in their ability to handle their responsibilities and do not continually worry about the reactions of superiors conceive of new problems as stimulating challenges and welcome frequent changes which prevent their jobs from becoming monotonous.*

Bureaucracy as Instrument of Innovation

In the large and complex societies of today, the implementation of new social policies requires bureaucratic machinery. Consider the case of inventions, which are sometimes viewed as spontaneous sources of social change, for example, the atomic bomb. To be sure, had Enrico Fermi and other scientists not had some brilliant ideas, there would be no atomic bomb, but these ideas alone did not bring it into existence. A complicated bureaucratic

* This situation probably also holds for teachers and other professions.

organization had to be set up both to produce atomic bombs and to furnish scientists with laboratories where they could work together on improvements and new developments. Not that all social change in modern society is bureaucratically instituted. New customs constantly arise without the intervention of bureaucracies. But the deliberate introduction of a social innovation on a large scale, whether it involves the production of a new weapon or the enforcement of a new law, depends on bureaucratic methods of administration.

Trade unions illustrate this point and some of its implications. For workers to realize their collective goal of improving their standard of living, they organized. To establish a strong labor union against the opposition of employers was, and still is, a very difficult task. It could not have been accomplished unless many workers, at least temporarily, had set aside their economic interests, often sacrificing their jobs and sometimes their very lives, because they were idealists whose primary objective was the creation of an effective labor organization. The need for such idealism in the establishment of trade unions was pointed out a century ago by Karl Marx, the man who is often assumed to interpret social conduct as determined primarily by economic interests and not by ideals. He wrote:

If the first aim of the general resistance was merely the maintenance of wages, combinations [of workers], at first isolated, constitute themselves into groups as the capitalists in their turn unite in the idea of repression, and in the face of always united capital, the maintenance of the association [union] becomes more necessary to them than that of wages. This is so true that the English economists are amazed to see the workers sacrifice a good part of their wages in favor of associations, which in the eyes of the economists, are established solely in favor of wages.[3]

Without using the term, Marx described in this passage the process of displacement of goals from high wages to maintenance of the organization. Observing the early struggles of the labor movement, he assumed this process to be highly beneficial for it. The findings of more recent studies of trade unions suggest that he was too optimistic, in this respect as in many others. Displacement of goals frequently results in a preoccupation with keeping the bureaucratic apparatus going at the expense of its basic objectives.

Robert Michels's famous study of labor unions and democratic parties in Germany at the beginning of the present century is concerned with this problem. Even a socialist party or a progressive union, regardless of how egalitarian its principles, must establish a hierarchical bureaucracy to put its reform program into effect. (The issues raised by this so-called "iron law of oligarchy" will be discussed in the next chapter.) The major interest of party or union officials is to strengthen the organization, not only because their jobs depend on its survival, but also because a powerful machine is needed in the fight for the intended reforms. In this respect, the self-interest of the leadership and the collective interest of the membership coincide. Officials, consequently, are willing to make great sacrifices for the sake of fortifying the organization. To attract more members, they will abandon unpopular points of the program. To prevent the possibility of a crushing defeat, they will fail to enforce union demands by calling a strike. "Thus, from a means, organization becomes an end." [4] Step by step, the original objectives are surrendered in the interest of increased organizational strength. The resulting organization may be extremely strong, but it is no longer an instrument for effecting the social reforms that were initially planned. What was once a socialist party (or a radical union) has turned into a rather con-

servative one. The inevitable fate of all reformist movements, according to Michels, is to grow conservative in the
course of becoming organized.

This conclusion has important implications that extend
far beyond the question of the future of socialism. The
radical ideas of the Reformation spread more or less spontaneously without the aid of a bureaucratic apparatus, producing profound changes in the institutional structure of
European society. Michels suggested that this cannot hap-
pen in today's bureaucratized societies. For new ideas to
find expression in institutional change, they must be bureaucratically implemented. In the process of creating an
effective bureaucratic apparatus, radical new ideas are always renounced in favor of more conservative ones. In
other words, people cannot possibly control their common
destiny by instituting desirable social reforms. For unless
they establish a bureaucratic organization for this purpose,
they will not be successful in realizing their new ideals,
and if they do, they will abandon them. There is reason
to assume, however, that this impasse is not entirely insurmountable. Although Michels analyzed a doubtlessly
prevalent feature of organizational life, he ignored another
trend that points in the opposite direction.

An examination of unions and parties that began with a
very radical program reveals, indeed, that most of those
that survived replaced their earlier radical goals by more
conservative ones and greater concern with administrative
matters in the course of establishing an effective organization. But study of unions that initially had more limited
plans for change discloses different tendencies. The American labor movement provides a good illustration. After
the decline seventy years ago of the Knights of Labor,
who had advocated a radical political program, most unions confined their efforts to the pursuit of two objectives:
establishing the right of collective bargaining and raising

wages. To be sure, concern with building a strong union sometimes pushed these two goals into the background, as jurisdictional strikes indicate, and some union leaders became increasingly conservative.[5] The main development, however, was not the one stressed by Michels: unions did not relinquish their original objectives. Quite the contrary, they achieved them in large part and strove for new, further-reaching reforms. Thus, the right of collective bargaining supplied a basis for the fight for workers' pensions, a social innovation far surpassing the aspirations of union members a few decades ago. This process, the reverse of displacement of goals, can be called "succession of goals"; as earlier objectives are attained, they become stepping stones for new ones.

The succession of goals, of course, is not primarily the result of the superior idealism of American as compared with German labor leaders, but the consequence of structural constraints in the organization. Once a union has achieved its major objectives, the enthusiasm of its members tends to wane. Many withdraw their support, financially and otherwise, and thereby threaten the persistence of the organization. The very fact that union officials are interested in maintaining their job and power constrains them to seek new ways of stimulating membership support. An effective method for recreating vigorous interest in union affairs is to establish new objectives for which workers are willing to fight. Hence, new goals often emerge in organizations as old ones have been reached. This is the case not only in unions but also in other organizations marked by bureaucracy's stamp.[6]

What determines whether displacement of goals or succession of goals predominates in an organization? This crucial question can be only partially answered. When the original objectives of a social movement arouse intense hostility and violent attacks, the insecurity of its members and their preoccupation with creating an organization and preserving it are likely to constrain them to compromise their ideals in order to avoid annihilation. When the community permits an organization, if only by default, to become established and attain at least some of its first objectives in a relatively short period, it will probably find new fields to conquer in the course of its development. How radical can social movements be without provoking hostilities that destroy them? How long is the period of grace before the struggle is given up as hopeless and the initial objectives are abandoned to maintain the organization? We do not yet know the answers to these questions, although a few recent researches provide suggestive leads to the study of interconnections between organizational factors and social change.

Conservative Pressures in Two Social Contexts

A brief review of two empirical investigations of progressive programs and their fate indicates the complex relationship between bureaucratic structures and changes in social policies. Whereas both studies found strains toward conservativism, the social forces responsible for them were quite different.

Philip Selznick's study of the Tennessee Valley Authority shows that the grass-roots policy adopted by this New Deal agency had unanticipated consequences that brought about fundamental changes in its progressive program.[7] The principle of grass-roots democracy emphasizes that the central government should not simply impose its authority upon the people in a region, but should give them a voice in the management of the federal agencies that affect their lives. Since all people in the Tennessee Valley could not directly participate in administrative decisions, this principle was implemented in actual practice by appointing representatives of powerful local institutions, notably the land-grant colleges, to positions on the policy-making body of the TVA. Many of these influential persons and organizations had been strongly opposed to the TVA, and their opposition might well have put serious obstacles in its way. The cooptation of representatives of these powerful conservative groups by the TVA, that is, their absorption into its leadership structure, averted this threat. The grass-roots method, as it was interpreted, constituted a mechanism that permitted a New Deal agency to function in a region dominated by conservative forces.

The initial commitment to work through locally established institutions brought about unforeseen effects that, paradoxically, contradicted the democratic spirit of the grass-roots doctrine that had been the reason for making the commitment. As men with conservative views who represented vested interests and not the majority of people in the area were appointed to its board of directors, TVA's policies became increasingly conservative and removed from New Deal principles. Thus, the TVA discriminated against Negroes; it came into conflict with other New Deal agencies, such as the Farm Security Administration; and various policies that had been designed to protect the public interest against special private interests were reversed. The last point is exemplified by the changes that occurred in the purchase of land for reservoirs. Building a reservoir improves the soil around it. To permit the public, whose funds paid for the reservoir, to benefit from this increment in land value, the TVA established the policy that the purchase of land for each reservoir include a surrounding protective strip 300 to 1,000 feet wide. Many landowners, anxious to reap these benefits themselves, were opposed to this program of public ownership.

Since their interest was represented on TVA's board, their pressure was successful. In 1942, the policy was reversed, the board of directors deciding "to limit the purchase of land for reservoir purposes to the minimum appropriate for the particular project," [8] which usually did not include any protective strip.

Selznick does not deny that the TVA produced profound changes in the Tennessee Valley and greatly contributed to the welfare of its economically deprived people. But he shows that these changes were not as far-reaching and not as unequivocally in the interest of the larger population in the area as had been originally planned. In the course of its development, the bureaucracy became more conservative.

S. M. Lipset, in his study of a socialist government in a Canadian province, also observes that the bureaucratic implementation of a progressive program occasioned its modification.[9] When the C.C.F. (Cooperative Commonwealth Federation) came into power in Saskatchewan in 1944 and its members took over all cabinet posts, they retained the former administrators of government bureaucracies as their deputies. Although it was known that most of the high government officials were middle-class persons not at all sympathetic to the socialist program of the C.C.F., the leaders held that they needed these administrative experts to operate the bureaucratic machinery in the various governmental departments. Moreover, ministers assumed that they would determine policy and that their deputies would only carry it out. In the process of being administered by conservative bureaucrats, however, socialist policies were often basically altered. Here are a few illustrations from Lipset's book:

> A number of civil servants were able to convince their ministers that certain changes were not administratively feasible or that they would incur too much opposition.

Some deputy ministers exchanged information with other deputies on their technique of controlling their ministers. . . . Some key officials boasted of "running my department completely," and of "stopping hare-brained radical schemes."

One cabinet minister, who has since discharged a large part of his field staff, found as a result of complaints from local members of the C.C.F. that members of his staff continued to grant leases and farming privileges to well-to-do persons who had secured them under previous governments, though it was now government policy to give them to poorer farmers and landless veterans.

One cabinet minister decided that certain government work that had previously been contracted out to private concerns should be done by government employees whenever possible. His deputy minister, however, continued sending the work out to private concerns.[10]

An important similarity marks the findings of Lipset and Selznick, but there is also a difference that, though less obvious, is no less important. If we focus our attention upon the political program, we notice the similarity. In both instances, a progressive program was modified in the course of being implemented by bureaucratic methods. If we focus our attention upon the bureaucratic organization, on the other hand, we can see that it played quite a different role in the two cases. In Saskatchewan, bureaucracies obstructed plans for reform that had originated elsewhere, whereas in Tennessee, external forces obstructed, partly through infiltration, the bureaucracy's original plans for reform. The fact that government policy was modified in a conservative direction in both cases reveals the power of conservative forces in Canadian and American society. In one case, however, conservative pressure was exercised *by* bureaucracies and its success indicates their strength, while in the other case, conservative pressures were exercised *upon* the bureaucracy and their success indicates its weakness.

It should be noted that neither study suggests that the bureaucratic structure itself generated the conservative trend. Selznick shows that in the case of the TVA it originated outside the bureaucracy, and Lipset stresses that in Saskatchewan it was due to the conservative orientation of the particular officials and not to inherent tendencies in the bureaucratic form of organization. Moreover, many parts of the progressive programs of the TVA and the C.C.F. were actually realized. Michels's conclusion that the bureaucratic machinery necessary for implementing new social ideals invariably destroys them is perhaps too pessimistic.

6

Bureaucracy and Democracy

To ASSESS bureaucracy's impact on democratic values, its internal and external consequences must be distinguished. Either we are concerned with the particular structures that are bureaucratically organized and raise the questions of whether this organizing principle is compatible with internal democracy and, if not, whether the bureaucratization of some organizations is nevertheless justified in a democracy; or we are concerned with the society within which numerous bureaucracies exist and raise the questions of whether they threaten its democratic institutions and, if so, how to protect democracy against this threat. Answers to the first two questions will furnish clues for answering the second two.

Bureaucracy's power of control has implications for its own members, on the one hand, and for society at large, on the other. In addition, it has implications for its clients, who constitute a border-line group, being neither fully

part of the organization nor completely external to it. At
the outset of this study, it was mentioned that the accusation of bureaucratic inefficiency, even when it is not
factually correct, reveals attitudes of clients toward bureaucracies that must be explained. An analysis of the
sources of such antagonistic attitudes can serve as an
introduction for the discussion of the other problems of
bureaucratic power.

The Accusation of "Red Tape"

There is no doubt that bureaucracies sometimes operate
inefficiently. When this occurs, however, clients rarely
have an opportunity to observe it. Conversely, many bureaucratic practices condemned by clients are not in fact
inefficient. For example, being required to fill out lengthy
forms in minute detail, including entries that are clearly
not pertinent to the particular case, is inconvenient from
the standpoint of the client but may be expedient for the
bureaucracy. This requirement is more efficient than permitting clients to decide which entries are relevant, since
even occasional omissions of pertinent information would
interfere with operations. Think of the last time you
accused some officials of being so entangled in red tape
that they could not work effectively. Was it after you had
made a careful investigation and obtained evidence that
given operating methods were disadvantageous *for the
bureaucracy?* More likely, it was when *you* felt disadvan-
taged by a bureaucratic decision, and you gave vent to
your powerless anger by leveling the accusation without
knowing whether inefficiency was involved or not. We all
do this—it makes us feel better.

The individual client stands helpless before the powerful bureaucracy, awaiting decisions that often vitally affect
his interests. Greatly concerned with his case, he sees in

it a number of exceptional circumstances that deserve special consideration, but the impersonal bureaucratic machinery disregards these and handles the case simply as one of a general category. Raging against adverse decisions or interminable delays is worse than futile, since it does not sway the impersonal organization and merely emphasizes one's impotence. Frustrated clients can relieve their pent-up aggression, however, in discussions of bureaucratic stupidity and red tape. Whereas the organization's ruthlessness, not its inefficiency, is the source of their antagonism, by expressing it in the form of an apparently disinterested criticism of performance, clients derive a feeling of superiority over the "blundering bureaucrats" that serves as a psychological compensation for being under their power. To be sure, we are incapable of direct retaliation when the actions of powerful bureaucracies hurt our interests, but we retaliate indirectly by contributing through our opinion and ridicule to the low public esteem of bureaucrats in our society.

Findings of a survey on attitudes toward bureaucratic red tape support this interpretation.[1] People who placed a high value on social equality were found to be more critical of red tape than those who did not. If this criticism were based entirely on factual observation, such a difference would probably not exist, since persons without an egalitarian orientation are as likely to have encountered bureaucratic inefficiency as those with one. If severe censure of red tape, on the other hand, is motivated by resentment against bureaucratic power, the reason for the difference becomes apparent: the more a person values equality, the more objectionable is the experience of being subjected to the controlling power of officials. The same principle can account for the finding that criticism of red tape was most pronounced among individuals who were particularly sensitive about their powerless position.

In the same study, "conservatives" were found to attach more importance to the problem of red tape than "radicals." (Respondents were divided into these two political camps on the basis of their attitudes toward labor unions.) This finding may seem surprising, inasmuch as radicals might be expected to be most eager to condemn the operations of the government and of private bureaucracies. This very fact, however, may explain their lesser inclination to worry about red tape. When a radical comes into conflict with power structures, this confirms his political conviction that existing institutions are unjust and should be changed. His radical ideology supplies a channel of aggression against the existing social system, obviating the need for expressing his aggression in other forms. But when a conservative comes into conflict with power structures, he is in a more difficult position. Since his ideology does not allow him to denounce the government and private enterprise, even when his interests have been injured by their actions, he often seeks to relieve his feelings of frustration through attacks on the administrative machinery and its red tape.

Implicit in the prevalent condemnation of red tape is a significant social consequence of this practice, which can be most clearly seen in totalitarian countries. In Soviet Russia, for instance, criticism of the government and its institutions is strictly prohibited with one notable exception. Sharp criticism of bureaucratic mismanagement and red tape is permitted and, indeed, encouraged, as indicated by its frequent appearance in the government-owned press. The dictatorship, through ruthless suppression and disregard for the public's interests, engenders considerable hostility, which might lead to attempts to overthrow it. Although the nature of government policies rather than lack of efficiency in their administration is the basis of this hostility, by providing an opportunity for releasing aggression in complaints about administrative red tape, the dictatorship reduces the danger that the people will rebel. But if this scapegoating serves an important function for a totalitarian regime, it is dysfunctional for a democratic society. Fuming against red tape and bureaucratic *methods* serves as a psychological substitute for opposition to bureaucratic *policies* that violate the interests of individuals. It therefore interferes with democratic processes, which presuppose that people are able and willing freely to express their opposition to existing power structures and their policies.

Contrasting Principles of Internal Control

Whatever the specific objectives of a bureaucratic organization, its formal purpose can be defined as the effective accomplishment of these objectives. This is the case for an army, for example, which is expected to win battles; for a factory, which is expected to produce goods that can be sold for a profit; for an employment agency, which is expected to find jobs for applicants and workers for employers. There is a second type of organization, however, which has no specific objectives but the purpose of furnishing mechanisms for establishing consensus on common objectives; the machinery of a democratic government is of this type. A third type, cited in Chapter One, consists of organizations designed to supply their members with intrinsic satisfactions either of a spiritual sort, as in a church, or of a secular nature, as in a social club. The following discussion is primarily concerned with the contrast between internal social control in the first two kinds of organization. Internal conditions in the third type, which will not be analyzed here, are more similar to those of the second than those of the first type.

Efficiency versus Dissent If an organization is established for the explicit purpose of realizing specified objectives, it is expected to be governed by the criterion of
efficiency. An organization so governed has been defined
as a bureaucracy. Defined in this way, the bureaucratic
form of organization is fundamentally different from both
the democratic and the autocratic forms. Neither the will
of the majority nor the personal choice of a ruler or a
ruling clique reigns supreme, but the rational judgment
of experts. Although both authoritarian elements and concessions to democratic values are found in bureaucratic
structures, efficiency is the ultimate basis for evaluating
whether such elements are appropriate. Disciplined obedience in the hierarchy of authority, ideally, is not valued
for its own sake, as it is in an autocracy, but is encouraged
to the extent to which it contributes to effective coordination and uniform operations. Similarly, while pronounced
inequalities are inherently opposed in a democracy, the
principal reason for minimizing them in a bureaucracy
is that they inhibit optimum performance. Bureaucratization implies that considerations of efficiency outweigh all
others in the formation and development of the organization.

But if men organize in order to ascertain the ideas that
prevail among them and then to agree on common objectives, their purpose requires that the basic principle which
governs their action is freedom of dissent. In this type of
democratic organization, considerations of efficiency are
expected to be subordinated to the central aim of stimulating the free expression of conflicting opinions. Of course,
democratic processes are not the most expeditious way of
arriving at decisions either for total societies or for limited
associations, such as trade unions. But the fact that it
would be more efficient if the leader were to decide on the
objectives to be pursued is irrelevant, since this policy

could not possibly accomplish the purpose of determining those objectives that are commonly agreed upon or express the view of the majority. To assure that the majority viewpoint remains supreme, a limitation has to be imposed on the majority itself. It must not stifle the opposition of any minority, however small its numbers or extreme its views, for unless dissenting voices can be heard today, tomorrow's decisions will not be democratic ones.

Bureaucratic and democratic structures can be distinguished, then, on the basis of the dominant organizing principle: efficiency or freedom of dissent. Each of these principles is suited for one purpose and not for another. When people set themselves the task of determining the social objectives that represent the interests of most of them, the crucial problem is to provide an opportunity for all conflicting viewpoints to be heard. In contrast, when the task is the achievement of given social objectives, the essential problem to be solved is to discover the efficient, not the popular, means for doing so. Democratic values require not only that social goals be determined by majority decision, but also that they be implemented through the most effective methods available, that is, by establishing organizations that are bureaucratically rather than democratically governed. The existence, therefore, of such bureaucracies does not violate democratic values. But these values are threatened by the encroachment of concern with bureaucratic efficiency upon those institutions where freedom of dissent is essential, where the guiding goal is to enable men to arrive at democratic decisions. Thus bureaucratic efficiency is expected to prevail in specialized government agencies, but not in the political arena. Various attempts to suppress radical political opposition in the interest of national security illustrate how efficiency considerations intrude upon freedom of dissent.

Democratic processes are in particular danger of being undermined by bureaucratization in organizations which have the double purpose of deciding on common objectives, on the one hand, and of carrying the decisions out, on the other. Political parties are a case in point. Large-scale democracy depends on the existence of opposing parties. They have the function of giving expression to the political beliefs of people and to serve as channels through which they can influence the government. To fulfill this responsibility, a party must be democratically organized, which means that primaries and other devices are used to assure that the party program reflects the wishes of its adherents. Democratic parties, however, also seek to win elections, which requires an efficient organization. Hence, they tend to be governed by political machines and national committees, primaries being relegated to a relatively inconsequential role. In order to make parties more effective instruments for winning victories, their function of permitting the voters to decide the political platforms between which they will choose at election time is sacrificed.

Incorporated business concerns furnish another illustration of this tendency. A clear distinction exists between the management of a business and the organization of its legal owners as stockholders in a public corporation. According to our laws and the principles of capitalism, it is presumed that the business is managed on the basis of efficiency, but that the board of directors of the corporation is democratically elected by the stockholders. The procedure employed for this purpose actually defeats its intent. Proxies are provided every stockholder, which give him about as much choice in elections as the citizen of a totalitarian nation. He has almost no way of opposing the existing leadership, since in most cases he can only endorse this group by signing the proxy or not vote at all.

(Any one stockholder can attend the annual meetings and voice his opposition, but all stockholders could not possibly do so. There is no stadium large enough to hold the one million people who own shares of the American Telephone and Telegraph Company or the hundreds of thousands who share the ownership of other large corporations.) In fact, therefore, most public corporations are dominated by a few officials, and the large majority of stockholders, sometimes owning more than 90 per cent of the shares, have no influence on management.[2] Only when a faction arises, as occurred among the stockholders of the New York Central Railroad in 1954, are there alternative slates of candidates for directorships from which to choose, and democratic processes are thus temporarily revived.[3]

This case suggests that the perpetuation of democratic processes depends on permanent factions, that is, opposition parties within the organization. The situation in labor unions, in this respect, is little different from that in business corporations. As long as factional strife prevails in a union, its members can throw their support to either side and therefore influence the policies of the organization; once it ceases, they no longer have this power. Factions rarely survive for more than brief periods, however, since the one that gains control typically fortifies its leadership position by suppressing the opposition. Such undemocratic action is often justified by the need of remaining united in the struggle with employers—internal disagreements weaken the union and must be avoided. Implicit in this argument is the assumption that the sole function of a union is to be an efficient instrument for attaining given objectives, such as higher wages, an assumption representing a very narrow conception of unionism. Labor unions are more broadly conceived as organizations that enable workers to have a voice in determining their employment and working conditions. There are various objectives that

a union can pursue; unless its members decide which of
these to seek at any given time the union does not represent
their interests. For this purpose, the union must establish
a democratic machinery and must protect it against the
threat of being destroyed for the sake of increased efficiency or strength. Let us examine how one union successfully maintained internal democracy.

A Union with Two Parties If internal democracy were
to incapacitate a union from being an effective bargaining
agent, workers could hardly be expected to engage in
such luxury. A recent study by Lipset and his colleagues
of the International Typographical Union shows, however,
that this development is not inevitably the case.[4] This
union, which is democratically governed, is a very strong
and effective representative of the interests of its members.

The democratic character of the I.T.U. manifests itself in
many ways. Most important is the fact that the officials of
the international union and of the larger locals are bi-
annually chosen in elections which are not purely symbolic
affairs where the membership merely endorses the existing
leadership. In many elections in the past—half of those in
the New York local, for instance—the incumbent officials
have been defeated. Changes in administration were usually accompanied by sharp reversals in union policy. Thus,
one administration favored arbitration with employers,
whereas the opposition advocated that union demands
should be enforced through strikes and adopted a more
militant strategy when it was elected. Since the membership of the union was able to choose between such contrast-
ing alternatives, it actually determined policy. Basic
changes in union regulations must be endorsed by referendum, and more often than not the proposals of the leadership have been defeated, a further indication of the

independent spirit and democratic power of the rank and file.

Probably the main source of internal democracy in the I.T.U. is its two-party system, which has been in existence for half a century. Institutionalized parties assure that there is always an organized opposition to the leadership and that voters are presented with distinct alternatives, without which democratic decisions in large groups are impossible. Even the referendum is not an effective democratic mechanism in the absence of an opposition party, which is interested in discussing the administration's proposals with the membership and in pointing out their faults. In one-party unions, where such critical discussions are rarely initiated, most members have no basis for opposing intricate proposals of their leadership, and a large majority usually endorses them. In sharp contrast to the situation in the I.T.U., the rank and file in one-party unions is not able to use the referendum to curb the power of its leaders.

Opposing parties create the organizational conditions necessary for democratic processes to prevail. Indeed, they do more. It is often held that the apathy of most union members (and of members of other voluntary associations) is an insurmountable obstacle to democratic self-government. When they even fail to attend union meetings, how can they assume responsibility for managing the affairs of the organization? They can not, of course, in this event. But the important question concerns the reasons for their apathy. In the majority of unions where the leadership makes all significant decisions, meetings are dull, since only routine business is conducted, and there is no incentive for attendance. The existence of an opposition party greatly alters the nature of such gatherings. It forces the leadership to present crucial issues for discussion, and,

furthermore, the controversies between opposition and
incumbent officials transform even discussions of less important topics into interesting contests. The union member
is not merely a spectator; he can actively participate in
the discussion and has a voice in deciding the contest
through his ballot. Parties are anxious to win converts, and
once a union member becomes a partisan, he has an
additional inducement for attending union meetings. (Lipset shows that I.T.U. members who belonged to a party
attended union meetings more regularly than those who did
not.) In these various ways, institutionalized parties lessen
apathy and stimulate interest in union politics, thereby
providing a firm foundation for participation in democratic
self-government.

What were the conditions that enabled the I.T.U., virtually alone among American unions, to establish and
maintain a democratic two-party system? One condition
was its strong position in the printing industry. The members of a weak union usually must devote all their efforts
to the struggle with employers and have little time or
energy left for creating a democratic machinery in their
organization. A second condition that contributed to
internal democracy was that independent local unions of
printers had existed for many years before they joined
together and formed the International Typographical Union in 1850. Several locals maintained considerable auton-
omy, and it was the opposition of certain strong locals to
the international administration that provided the original
impetus for organizing a formal opposition party at the
beginning of this century. Thirdly, printers enjoy a fairly
high income, not much less than that of their union officials, and they generally like their work. While union
leaders whose status is far superior to that of the workers
under their jurisdiction often view defeat in election and
the necessity to return to work in a shop as an unbearable

calamity, I.T.U. officials do not. The latter, therefore, are less prone to try to prevent defeat at all costs, including the cost of sabotaging democratic methods. Attempts to undermine the two-party system are also discouraged by a fourth condition, namely, that the democratic tradition has become part of the value orientation of I.T.U. members. Officials are deterred from disregarding democratic processes, since such conduct would be strongly resented by the membership and invite defeat at the elections.

Finally, the members of the I.T.U. have created a large number of voluntary associations within their union, such as athletic organizations, lodges, social clubs, and the like. Printers spend much of their recreational life with other printers, partly because they often work at night and their leisure hours do not coincide with those of most people. These nonpolitical associations of printers promote interest in union politics and participation in democratic self-government on a wide scale. Printers who are unconcerned with the political affairs of the union usually belong to clubs where they come into contact with fellow craftsmen, some of whom are sufficiently interested in union politics to talk about such matters on every occasion, even when bowling or playing cards. In other words, the recreational associations of printers expose apathetic union members to discussions that are likely to stimulate increased concern with the union and the way it is managed. Moreover, the large number of voluntary organizations furnishes an opportunity for many union members to acquire the political skills involved in the administration of a democratic group. These men constitute a pool of experienced democratic administrators, from which the officials of the two parties and the leaders of the union can be drawn. The widespread active participation in both the political and recreational affairs of the I.T.U. sustains the internal democracy that the two-party system makes possible.

A Challenge for Democracy

In conclusion, let us briefly examine some implications of the prevalence of bureaucracies for democratic institutions. Strangely enough, social scientists who advance diametrically opposed theories about the historical development of bureaucratization agree on this point. One interpretation holds that the proliferation of bureaucracies is the result of modern capitalism. The economic advantages of large-scale production lead to the establishment of huge industrial enterprises and ultimately to monopolization. These powerful private bureaucracies put pressure on the government to safeguard their interests, for example, by enacting protective-tariff laws and setting up the bureaucratic apparatus necessary for enforcing them. Hence, bureaucracy in government as well as in private industry is the product of forces generated by capitalism.[5] Several liberal economists, in contrast, attribute the trend toward bureaucratization to the wilful effort of governments to interfere with the capitalist economy. If the government assumes the task of regulating economic life, it must greatly expand its bureaucratic machinery, disturbing the competitive mechanism of the free market and thereby facilitating the development of monopolies. The emergence of bureaucratic business monopolies as well as government bureaucracies is the inevitable outcome of the political decision to meddle with free enterprise.[6] The authors who advance these conflicting theses about the historical origins of large-scale bureaucracy, however, are in agreement concerning its consequences. Bureaucratization concentrates power in the hands of a few men and curtails the freedom of individuals that is essential for democracy.[7]

Bureaucracies endanger democratic freedoms, but at the same time they serve important functions in a democratic society that must not be ignored. Thus Weber points out that bureaucratic personnel policies—employment on the basis of technical qualifications—reduce the handicap of underprivileged groups in the competition for jobs. Negroes, for example, have a better chance of being hired when objective criteria rather than personal considerations govern the selection of candidates. Of course, the children of wealthier families, who can more easily afford the education that qualifies them for the most desirable jobs, continue to have a distinct advantage over others. Bureaucratization does not produce complete equality of occupational opportunities. Nevertheless, the fact that it does minimize the direct effects of status privileges, such as noble birth or skin color, constitutes a democratizing influence.

"Equal justice under law" is a fundamental democratic principle. The executive agencies which help to administer the law as well as the courts, according to this principle, must not discriminate against any person or group. Administrative officials who investigate legal violations have to interpret the law as they apply it to specific cases. Their judgment is usually not appealed to the courts and consequently assumes quasi-judicial significance. Unless all investigators interpret a law in the same manner, some persons will be treated more strictly than others. Hence, the decisions of all enforcement agents should be governed by uniform standards and protected against being influenced by personal considerations. This is another way of saying that bureaucratically organized enforcement agencies are necessary for all members of the society to be equal under the law.

Other contributions of bureaucracy have already been discussed. Democratic objectives would be impossible of attainment in modern society without bureaucratic organizations to implement them. Thus, once the decision to provide free employment service to the public had been reached through democratic processes, a complex administrative system for this purpose had to be established. Furthermore, the high standard of living we enjoy today depends, in part, on the adoption of efficient bureaucratic methods of organization in private industry. Whereas, in theory, a low standard of living does not inhibit democracy, in actual practice it does. Large parts of the population lose interest in preserving political freedoms if they are preoccupied with finding ways to satisfy their minimum economic wants. Under these conditions, people are least likely to participate in their democratic government (economically deprived persons are, in fact, less prone to exercise their right to vote than others) and most likely to fall prey to demagogues who promise them some relief from their economic misery.

Were it not for these services rendered by bureaucracies for a democratic society, their existence would not pose a dilemma, only a problem. In such a case, the task would still be difficult, but the decision would be clear: to endeavor by all means to abolish bureaucracies, because they have serious dysfunctions for democracy. First of all, bureaucracies create profound inequalities of power. They enable a few individuals, those in control of bureaucratic machinery, to exercise much more influence than others in the society in general and on the government in particular. This huge differential in political and social power violates the democratic principles that sovereignty rests with all and that each citizen has an equal voice.

The prevalence of bureaucracies in a society also undermines democracy in more subtle ways. Lipset suggests that the existence of smaller self-governing bodies, the voluntary associations, is of crucial significance for democracy in the I.T.U. They provide experience in democratic participation, stimulate concern with the political affairs of the union, and lessen the apathy that often characterizes the members of a large organization, who feel remote from its administration. In a society with more than one thousand times the membership of the I.T.U., the United States, democratic intermediary organizations would appear to be even more important for self-government in the larger social structure. Tocqueville made this observation over a century ago in his classic work *Democracy in America*. Since his time, however, many formerly democratic organizations have become bureaucratized. We generally no longer govern our voluntary associations: we simply join them, pay our dues, and let experts run them. As a result, we have less and less opportunity for acquiring experiences that are essential for effective participation in democratic government.

A person must be able to communicate his ideas to others if he is to influence public opinion. But in a community the size of the United States, the individual's voice is lost, and only organized groups have the strength to make themselves heard. By joining democratic organizations and helping to decide their policies, people have a chance to exert some influence on the larger community. The trend toward bureaucratization in all kinds of large organizations blocks this vital source of democratic influence.

The proliferation of bureaucracies, then, threatens democracy in various ways. But even if we could abolish them, we would be reluctant to do so, because we do not wish to surrender the benefits we derive from them. Some authors have concluded that modern society's need for bureaucratic methods spells the inevitable doom of democracy. But why interpret a historical dilemma as a sign of an inescapable fate? Why not consider it a challenge to find ways to avert the impending threat? If we want to utilize efficient bureaucracies, we must find democratic methods of controlling them lest they enslave us.

This is not an easy undertaking. Its accomplishment may well depend on democratic participation on a far wider scale than has ever been known. Perhaps, the challenge posed by bureaucratization can be met only if all citizens are able and motivated to devote a considerable portion of their time and energy to activities in the political life of their communities. Such a suggestion would have been unrealistic a century or two ago, when most men had to spend most of their waking hours making a living. The efficiency of the very bureaucracies against which we should protect democratic institutions, however, has reduced enormously the working week and increased the number of hours people have at their free disposal. Therefore, for the first time in history, all men, not merely a privileged few, are freed, if they choose, to take their duties as democratic citizens seriously. And as the level of popular education is raised, more people are becoming interested in political affairs. Many problems still lie ahead, as we all know. The full realization of democracy in modern society is a gigantic task. But would it not be a pity to give up in despair just when the tools needed for completing it seem to be in our hands?

FOOTNOTES

CHAPTER 1

1. See Pitirim Sorokin, *Social and Cultural Dynamics,* New York: American Book Company, 1937-1941. The author traces fluctuations in cultural emphasis on science and rationality, on the one hand, and faith and supernatural phenomena, on the other, from the earliest times to the present, and vigorously condemns the present trend toward rationalization.

2. *Capital,* Vol. I, Chaps. 26 to 31.

3. See Kenneth Boulding, *The Organizational Revolution,* New York: Harper & Brothers, 1953.

4. *From Max Weber: Essays in Sociology,* translated by H. H. Gerth and C. Wright Mills, New York: Oxford University Press, 1946, p. 228.

5. *Ibid.,* p. 232.

6. For a fuller discussion of this point, see Charles H. Page, "Bureaucracy and the Liberal Church," *The Review of Religion* 17:137-50 (1952).

CHAPTER 2

1. *From Max Weber: Essays in Sociology,* translated by H. H. Gerth and C. Wright Mills, New York: Oxford University Press, 1946, p. 196. By permission.

2. Max Weber, *The Theory of Social and Economic Organization,* translated by A. M. Henderson and Talcott Parsons, New York: Oxford University Press, 1947, p. 331.

3. *Ibid.,* p. 330.

4. *Ibid.,* p. 340.

5. *Ibid.,* p. 334.

6. *Ibid.,* p. 337.

7. *From Max Weber: Essays in Sociology, op. cit.,* p. 214.

8. Robert K. Merton, *Social Theory and Social Structure,* Glencoe, Ill.: Free Press, 1949, pp. 21-81.

9. For a general discussion of functional analysis, see Ely Chinoy, *Sociological Perspective: Basic Concepts and Their Application* (Studies in Sociology), New York: Random House, Inc., 1954, Chap. 5.

10. Chester I. Barnard, *The Functions of the Executive,* Cambridge: Harvard University Press, 1948, p. 123.

11. *From Max Weber: Essays in Sociology, op. cit.,* pp. 256-57. The advanced student will have recognized the indebtedness of the foregoing discussion to Weber's (pp. 204-16). It goes without saying that Weber's fund of historical knowledge and his profound theoretical insights about bureaucracy can be acknowledged as outstanding contributions in the field even if one rejects his use of the ideal-type construct.

12. For a fuller discussion of the unintended effects of Protestantism, see Elizabeth K. Nottingham, *Religion and Society* (Studies in Sociology), New York: Random House, Inc., 1954, pp. 50 ff.

13. Alvin W. Gouldner, *Patterns of Industrial Bureaucracy,* Glencoe, Ill.: Free Press, 1954.

14. *Ibid.,* pp. 97-98.

CHAPTER 3

1. Charles H. Page, "Bureaucracy's Other Face," *Social Forces* 25:89-91 (1946). By permission.

2. Condensed from *The Human Group* by George C. Homans, copyright, 1950, by Harcourt, Brace & Co., pp. 54-55, 66, 68-72. The empirical study of the Bank Wiring Observation Room, which Homans summarizes in this book and in which he participated, is fully reported in F. J. Roethlisberger and William J. Dickson, *Management and the Worker,* Cambridge: Harvard University Press, 1946, pp. 379-548.

3. Peter M. Blau, *The Dynamics of Bureaucracy,* Chicago: University of Chicago Press, 1955, pp. 99, 104-6, 108-11, 113. (Copyright, 1955, by the University of Chicago. Reprinted by permission of the University of Chicago Press.)

4. See, for instance, Roethlisberger and Dickson, *op. cit.,* pp. 3-186, and Elton Mayo, *The Human Problems of an Industrial Civilization,* New York: Macmillan Company, 1933.

5. See Frederick W. Taylor, *The Principles of Scientific Management,* New York: Harper & Brothers, 1911.

6. Wilbert E. Moore, *Industrial Relations and the Social Order,* New York: Macmillan Company, 1947, p. 190.

7. For a full discussion of this case, see Blau, *op. cit.,* pp. 49-67.

CHAPTER 4

1. Daniel Katz, Nathan MacCoby, and Nancy C. Morse, *Productivity, Supervision and Morale in an Office Situation,* Ann Arbor: Institute for Social Research, University of Michigan, 1950, especially pp. 17, 21, 29.

2. See, for instance, F. J. Roethlisberger and William J. Dickson, *Management and the Worker,* Cambridge: Harvard University Press, 1946, pp. 452-53.

3. For a clear illustration of this point in a street corner gang, see William F. Whyte, *Street Corner Society,* Chicago: University of Chicago Press, 1943, pp. 257-62.

4. For discussions of professional authority, see Talcott Parsons, *The Social System,* Glencoe, Ill.: Free Press, 1951, pp. 428-79; the same author's introduction to Max Weber, *The Theory of Social and Economic Organization,* translated by A. M. Henderson and Talcott Parsons, New York: Oxford University Press, 1947, pp. 58-59, n. 4; and Alvin W. Gouldner, *Patterns of Industrial Bureaucracy,* Glencoe, Ill.: Free Press, 1954, pp. 21-23.

5. See Peter M. Blau, *The Dynamics of Bureaucracy,* Chicago: University of Chicago Press, 1955, pp. 33-48.

CHAPTER 5

1. Walter R. Sharp, *The French Civil Service: Bureaucracy in Transition,* New York: Macmillan Company, 1931, pp. 446-50 (by permission); reprinted in Robert K. Merton, Ailsa P. Gray, Barbara Hockey, and Hanan C. Selvin (eds.), *Reader in Bureaucracy,* Glencoe, Ill.: Free Press, 1952, pp. 407-9.

2. Robert K. Merton, *Social Theory and Social Structure,* Glencoe, Ill.: Free Press, 1949, pp. 154-55. By permission.

3. Karl Marx, *The Poverty of Philosophy,* New York, International Publishers, n.d., p. 145; quoted in Reinhard Bendix

and Seymour M. Lipset, *Class, Status and Power,* Glencoe, Ill.: Free Press, 1953, p. 31.

4. Robert Michels, *Political Parties,* Glencoe, Ill.: Free Press, 1949, p. 373.

5. See Alvin W. Gouldner, "Attitudes of 'Progressive' Trade-Union Leaders," *American Journal of Sociology* 52:389-92 (1947).

6. See Peter M. Blau, *The Dynamics of Bureaucracy,* Chicago: University of Chicago Press, 1955, pp. 194-96.

7. Philip Selznick, *TVA and the Grass Roots,* Berkeley and Los Angeles: University of California Press, 1949.

8. *Ibid.,* p. 204.

9. S. M. Lipset, *Agrarian Socialism,* Berkeley and Los Angeles: University of California Press, 1950, pp. 255-75. By permission.

10. *Ibid.,* pp. 263, 265, 266-67.

CHAPTER 6

1. Alvin W. Gouldner, "Red Tape as a Social Problem," in Robert K. Merton, Ailsa P. Gray, Barbara Hockey, and Hanan C. Selvin (eds.), *Reader in Bureaucracy,* Glencoe, Ill.: Free Press, 1952, pp. 410-18.

2. Adolf A. Berle, Jr., and Gardiner C. Means, *The Modern Corporation and Private Property,* New York: Macmillan Company, 1932.

3. For a recent discussion of the bureaucratization of industry and trade, see Wilbert E. Moore, *Economy and Society* (Studies in Sociology), New York: Random House, Inc., 1955, Chap. 3.

4. S. M. Lipset, Martin Trow, and James Coleman, *Union Democracy* (Glencoe, Ill.: Free Press, 1956).

5. See Franz Neumann, *Behemoth,* New York: Oxford University Press, 1942; and Robert A. Brady, *Business as a System of Power,* New York: Columbia University Press, 1943.

6. See Ludwig von Mises, *Bureaucracy,* New Haven: Yale University Press, 1946; and Friederich von Hayek, *The Road to Serfdom,* Chicago: University of Chicago Press, 1944.

7. For a full discussion of the points made in this paragraph and a criticism of the two theories mentioned, see Reinhard Bendix, "Bureaucracy and the Problem of Power," *Public Administration Review* 5:194-209 (1945).

SELECTED READINGS

Basic source book

ROBERT K. MERTON, AILSA P. GRAY, BARBARA HOCKEY, and HANAN C. SELVIN (eds.), *Reader in Bureaucracy,* Glencoe, Ill.: Free Press, 1952.

Selections from the classics, such as Weber and Michels, and many pertinent studies of a more recent vintage. Includes a bibliography.

Theories of bureaucracy and organization

From Max Weber: Essays in Sociology, translated by H. H. Gerth and C. Wright Mills, New York: Oxford University Press, 1946.

Contains the classic essay on bureaucracy as well as essays on discipline, power, and authority which are pertinent to the discussions in this study. The translators provide an introduction to Weber's life and his writings.

MAX WEBER, *The Theory of Social and Economic Organization,* translated by A. M. Henderson and Talcott Parsons, New York: Oxford University Press, 1947.

The typology of authority in this book includes another general discussion of bureaucracy which is not as complete but somewhat more concise and clearer than that in the volume above.

ROBERT MICHELS, *Political Parties,* Glencoe, Ill.: Free Press, 1949.

There is no reason to agree with Michels's conclusion that democracy is hardly more than a utopian dream, but there are good reasons for reading his incisive analysis of parties and trade unions. Unless we learn to understand why democracy often does not work, how can we learn to make it work better?

CHESTER I. BARNARD, *The Functions of the Executive,* Cambridge: Harvard University Press, 1938.

An analysis of principles of organization in business by a former executive of a large company, who was one of the first to stress the importance of informal organization.

HERBERT A. SIMON, *Administrative Behavior,* New York: Macmillan Company, 1945.

A stimulating text on principles of administration, which views them as limits of the process of decision-making.

Case studies of bureaucracies

F. J. ROETHLISBERGER and WILLIAM J. DICKSON, *Management and the Worker,* Cambridge: Harvard University Press, 1939.

The famous study of informal organization in a variety of small work groups at the Hawthorne Works of the Western Electric Company.

PHILIP SELZNICK, *TVA and the Grass Roots,* Berkeley and Los Angeles: University of California Press, 1949.

Study of the way in which initial commitments of an organization to the existing power structure affected its operations in unintended ways.

ALVIN W. GOULDNER, *Patterns of Industrial Bureaucracy,* Glencoe, Ill.: Free Press, 1954.

Empirical study of the forces that engendered bureaucratization and its consequences in an industrial concern.

PETER M. BLAU, *The Dynamics of Bureaucracy,* Chicago: University of Chicago Press, 1955.

Study of interpersonal relationships in two government agencies with special emphasis on the analysis of processes of bureaucratic change.

S. M. LIPSET, MARTIN TROW, and JAMES COLEMAN, *Union Democracy* (Glencoe, Ill.: Free Press, 1956).

Historical and sociological study of both the bureaucratic and democratic features of the International Typographical Union. (See also Lipset's "The Political Process in Trade Unions," Chapter 4 in Morroe Berger, Theodore Abel, and Charles H. Page (eds.): *Freedom and Control in Modern Society,* New York: D. Van Nostrand, Inc., 1954.)